he

Psychic

Reality

Also by Robert Cracknell

Clues to the Unknown

the

Psychic

Reality

*Developing Your
Natural Abilities*

Robert
Cracknell

for the evolving human spirit HAMPTON ROADS
PUBLISHING COMPANY, INC.

Cover design by Marjoram Productions
Cover art by Nick Gonzalez

For information write:

Hampton Roads Publishing Company, Inc.
134 Burgess Lane
Charlottesville, VA 22902

Or call: 804-296-2772
FAX: 804-296-5096
e-mail: hrpc@hrpub.com
Web site: http://www.hrpub.com

If you are unable to order this book from your local
bookseller, you may order directly from the publisher.
Quantity discounts for organizations are available.
Call 1-800-766-8009, toll-free.

Library of Congress Catalog Card Number: 99-71618

ISBN 1-57174-132-1

10 9 8 7 6 5 4 3 2 1

Printed on acid-free recycled paper in Canada

Dedication

This book is dedicated to many people:

*to Andrew, who was responsible for ending my six-year
sabbatical and becoming an integral part of my life;*

to my good friend and mentor, Colin Wilson;

*to the Rainbow Men, whom I hope you will meet in the
very near future;*

*to Ian and Patrick for their technical expertise, with
special thanks;*

and most important—with love—to my Jenny.

Contents

The Psychic Safe Challenge

Robert Cracknell has conducted what he believes is a unique psychic experiment for this book. During the preparation of this book, he has psychically impregnated the same four-figure combination number into each and every one of its pages. He firmly believes that by the time the reader gets to the end of the book, he or she will be able to "pick up" his psychic safe combination number.

Will he be proved right?

The object is to not concentrate too hard. On completion of the book and exercises, test yourself, and then check the answer on page 167.

Introduction

Who Is Bob Cracknell?

In November 1980, the London publishers Hamlyn invited me to join them for lunch with my old friend Bob Cracknell. They had just accepted his *Clues to the Unknown*, subtitled "The Autobiography of a Psychic Detective," in which Bob told the story of some of his amazing cases.

Six years earlier, an unknown sadist who became known as "the Yorkshire Ripper" had killed his first victim—a prostitute named Wilma McCann—in Leeds and then stabbed her in the stomach, chest, and genital area. Thereafter, he killed eleven more women in the north of England.

During the lunch, I mentioned that the police had been to interview me concerning the Ripper murders—apparently a book of mine entitled *The Killer* had been quoted in one of the letters written to the police and signed "The Yorkshire Ripper." At this point, Bob commented that he had had an "intuition" that the Ripper would kill just once more, in two weeks time, that this would be his last killing, and that he would be arrested shortly after as a result of a routine traffic enquiry. I advised Bob to place his prophesy on record with a friend at the Oxford Society of Psychical Research.

A week later, on November 17, 1980, Jacqueline Hill, a Leeds university student, was murdered by the Ripper when she was on her way back to her lodgings. Her body was found the next morning.

On December 14, 1980, Bob was reported in the *Sunday Mirror* as saying he was convinced the Yorkshire Ripper lived in Bradford.

One Sunday evening, Bob was staying with us in Cornwall overnight. The telephone rang; it was his wife, Jenny, who wanted to tell him that the police had arrested a man in the red-light area of Sheffield, and that serious charges had been preferred against him the day following his arrest. The man lived in Bradford.

In fact, the police had picked up Peter Sutcliffe, the Yorkshire Ripper, when Sutcliffe was with another prostitute in a car stopped by the police, and in the course of routine questioning concerning the car, had discovered he was in possession of a hammer and a knife. Two days later, Sutcliffe admitted to the thirteen murders of the Yorkshire Ripper.

Ever since I had known Bob, he had had these sudden strange flashes of intuition. On one occasion, it had almost led to his arrest on a murder charge. In February 1977, a pretty blonde named Janie Shepherd had disappeared in the early evening in Queensway, London. Her red Mini was found abandoned a few days later. On April 18, 1977, her body was found on a common called No Man's Land near St. Albans. A journalist who had recently interviewed Bob rang him and asked him casually if he had any feelings about the Janie Shepherd mystery. Bob himself writes: "Now, as he asked me the question, I was suddenly 'involved.' Vibrations and impressions began flooding into my brain. I had a clear image of a Mini car, and there, on the back seat, was a contraceptive device. I knew that it had been torn from inside her in the course of the sexual attack." Bob told his journalist friend, and the next morning he received a visit from two detectives of the murder squad, who were convinced that he was the killer. The piece of evidence about the contraceptive device had been kept from the general public, and the police were convinced that only Janie's murderer could have known about it. It took Bob some time to convince them that he was a psychic, and this kind of thing often happened to him.

As the police were leaving, Bob suddenly had another flash of intuition. He said: "By the way, I get a strong feeling that the killer was a black man with a scar on one cheek, and that you have him in custody already." The two detectives looked at one another, and Bob immediately knew that they felt he was right.

Eleven years later, a man from Barbados named David Lashley, who had a scar on one cheek and who was serving twelve years for rape, told a fellow prisoner: "If I'd killed her (the girl he raped) as I killed Janie Shepherd, I wouldn't be here now." He then described the murder to his fellow prisoner in some detail. The man told a warden, with the result that, on the day of his release, Lashley was rearrested. At the moment, he is serving life imprisonment for the murder of Janie Shepherd.

These cases offer some idea of what I mean when I say that Bob Cracknell is one of the most remarkable psychics of the twentieth century. But they only give an example of what he can do when operating on the purely practical level. (In fact, he formed and operated a major investigation agency, his clients being every major banking and financial institution in the U.K.) But Bob is far more than a psychic in this rather down-to-earth sense. He has been tested by psychical researchers and has revealed powers far more unusual than those of "second sight." In the early 1970s, the youth committee of the Oxford Spiritualist Church decided to put Cracknell to one of the most difficult tests ever devised—a test of his power to foresee the future. Before a Spiritualist meeting, Bob was asked to sit on the platform and to predict which member of the audience, who had still not arrived, would take a particular chair. Bob not only wrote a description of a girl, but he also included details about her personal life. In due course, a girl sat in the chair and then went on to confirm that all the details Cracknell had provided about her personal life were correct.

A young Oxford student at a later meeting, Kevin McClure, who was interested in psychic research, had Bob submit to a far more stringent test. In case Bob at the earlier meeting had caught a glimpse of the girl—the audience was preparing to file in as he made his prediction—he was asked to describe who would sit in a certain chair three hours before the meeting. Looking at the empty chair, Bob once again experienced a flood of impressions, which he tried to write down as quickly as he could, covering page after page. He felt that the person who would sit on the chair would be a young man and that he was somehow connected with an older man named George as well as with a country lane that led up to a farm. Three hours later, the young man sat in the chair and admitted both that Bob's comments were 80 percent accurate and that George was his grandfather, who had worked on the farm that Bob had described.

In due course, Kevin McClure wrote to me and suggested that I ought to meet Bob. He told me the story of the "empty chair test" and I was fascinated. I was at the time editing a series of books on the paranormal, and the publisher was giving a launching party at the Cheshire Cheese in Fleet Street. Bob came along to the party, and we met in the crowded room. I saw a powerfully built man who looked more like a boxer than a clairvoyant and who talked in a purposeful, assertive way. But we had no chance to have a real conversation, and I asked him to come around to meet me the next day for lunch. He arrived with a pretty girl named Jenny—his wife—and he looked rather exhausted. It seemed he had spent the whole night sitting up drinking with a painter friend of mine and had not got to bed until dawn. And he had been so bored and nauseated by the literary party that he had decided not to bother to come to lunch—but Jenny had persuaded him to change his mind.

I later came to realize that this was typical of Bob. Anyone who has formed a picture of clairvoyants from Madam Arcati in Noel Coward's *Blithe Spirit* would find Cracknell a refreshing—and possibly traumatic—experience. He is totally down-to-earth, blunt, aggressive, and impatient; he is also intelligent, honest, and obsessively—almost self-destructively—devoted to his own vision of the truth.

I learned from him that this had made him very unpopular in Spiritualist circles. His remarkable psychic powers had meant that he had been in great demand at Spiritualist meetings. But he felt that "clairvoyance" was simply a perfectly normal faculty that all human beings possess and that we simply have to awaken in ourselves. He was disinclined to believe in life after death—and certainly disinclined to believe that his remarkable powers proved anything about "the other side." His outspokenness had caused many Spiritualist churches to drop him.

At the time I met Bob, it seemed to me that he was probably correct—or, at least, that the questions of whether human beings live on as "spirits" after death, is completely irrelevant. I certainly had no sympathy whatever with people who went to Spiritualist meetings, or for "sittings" with mediums, in the hope of getting in touch with dead loved ones. However, since then, I have been forced to look far more closely into the question of survival after death. First, I wrote a book about poltergeists, which convinced me that poltergeists are spirits, not the unconscious minds of disturbed adolescents; and second, I was then asked to write a book called *Afterlife*, which finally convinced me that the evidence for life after death is overwhelming. But even this seems to me, in a sense, fairly unimportant. The real problem for human beings is to learn what to do with their lives.

And it seemed to me that what Bob Cracknell was saying was highly relevant to this question. He was saying that we possess far greater powers than we realize, and that we can train ourselves to make use of them.

But if we all possess them, then why do we not make use of them as a matter of course? The answer is interesting. Very few of us realize what we are capable of doing. After he had been sentenced to thirty years imprisonment, the gangster Ronnie Kray began painting. He soon discovered that he was an unusually talented painter. If he had been born into a middle-class family, and given a paint box when he was a child, he might well have discovered his talent early, gone off to art school, and ended as a distinguished modern painter instead of a murderer. Few of us actually have any idea of what unknown powers we might possess.

Now, where clairvoyants are concerned, I noted a long time ago that many of them seemed to have had a fairly traumatic childhood, or have had some sudden shock that seemed to release their powers. The Dutch clairvoyant Peter Hurkos was a housepainter until he fell off a ladder and fractured his skull so badly that he almost died. When he was recovering in the hospital, he suddenly realized that he had developed "second sight"; he often had a sudden insight into the private life of someone he was talking to, particularly if there was any physical contact, such as shaking hands. Uri Geller once told me that when he was a small child, his mother was using a sewing machine, and he was fascinated by a hole in the base of the machine, in the bottom of which he could see a small spark. He thrust his finger into the machine while she was using it and received a shock that knocked him backwards. He dates his psychic powers from this event.

Bob Cracknell's childhood was exceptionally lonely and emotion-starved, as he reveals in his autobiography. A child with many playmates, and plenty to think about, remains concentrated on the world of the five senses. A lonely child, if he is not to die of boredom, needs to learn to make use of his inner powers. I was a lonely child myself—mainly because I simply didn't enjoy joining in children's games—and I compensated by reading everything I could lay my hands on. Bob is not that type. He is basically a man of action. If his childhood had been normal and happy, I imagine that he might have quickly become the captain of the school football team, chairman of the debating society, or head prefect. And if his parents had been well-to-do, he would have been sent to public school, then to Sandhurst, and might have made an excellent soldier. Born in America around 1880, he would surely have found his way to Alaska in the gold rush.

Instead, he was the illegitimate son of a cockney girl. For the first five years of his life he was fostered, being brought up by a woman who was not his mother; then at the outbreak of war, he was evacuated to Nottingham, where he was kept half-starved and was beaten for bed-wetting. A less vital and resilient child would have become passive and miserable and probably would have remained that way for the rest of his life. Bob was a natural fighter. And it was at this point that he began to develop a deeper kind of sensitivity than did the people around him.

Yet, oddly enough, he did not realize that he was "psychic" until he went into the Royal Air Force for his national service. One night, when he was NCO-in-charge, he went to sleep on a bunk, arranging with one of the men that he should be awakened immediately if the orderly officer appeared.

Then, suddenly, he felt that he could hear the voice of the orderly officer asking where he was. He struggled to wake up but was unable to move. He was aware that this was not a dream. He was definitely not asleep. Yet he was paralyzed. At that moment, he felt that one of the men had come into the room to shake him awake. He managed to force himself into wakefulness—and realized that the room was empty. A few minutes later, somebody did enter the room to warn him that the guard commander was approaching.

So many psychics have described this experience of paralysis that I have come to believe that it is a sign that the physical body and the "spirit," or astral body—or whatever you want to call it—are slightly "out of sync." It is as if you are sitting in the driving seat of a car, but the seat is too far back for your feet to reach the pedals.

Even so, Bob was not yet fully aware that he was psychic. It took several years—and some extremely painful experiences—before he began to develop his psychic powers.

Another friend of mine, the writer Stan Gooch, was a lecturer in psychology at a provincial university when he was invited to attend a Spiritualist seance. He went out of curiosity, and halfway through the meeting, he experienced a sudden roaring sound in his ears, followed by complete loss of consciousness. When he woke up, he learned that he had gone into a trance and that various "spirits" had spoken through his mouth.

Clearly, this would seem to be a faculty that some people possess and some people don't.

But I have come to believe that this conclusion is a mistake. Bob pointed out to me that even people who regard themselves as completely nonpsychic sometimes experience an odd sense of "knowing" something—for example, going into a room with a husband and wife and realizing that they have been having a violent quarrel just before you arrived.

And then, what about our intuitive feelings about certain people? Twenty years ago, the headmaster of a local junior school wrote to me telling me that he had written a book and asking me if I could spare the time to read it. It was a highly talented piece of work, but it was too unprofessional to be accepted by a publisher. Encouraged by me, he went on to write several more novels, which got steadily better, yet which never quite reached the level of being publishable.

Whenever I met him, I always felt there was something about him that worried me a little. Although he was amiable enough, you got the impression that he was the sort of person that never looked you straight in the eye. There was a kind of underlying uncertainty about him, a certain lack of self-assurance which was strange in a headmaster.

Then, quite suddenly, we were all startled and rather shocked to hear that he had been arrested for sexually assaulting his pupils. Apparently he had been doing it for years. He would invite girls—and boys—into his study and then proceed to fondle them, often getting to the point of sexual intercourse.

The scandal, of course, ruined his career, and he later died of AIDS. But I always felt that there was something "a bit odd" about him, without ever being able to put my finger on it. Was I being "psychic," or was this just the kind of intuition that we all possess?

Bob Cracknell would claim that this is a false distinction. We all possess more psychic ability than we realize, and we make use of it all the time—without realizing what we are doing.

Now it strikes me that if this is true—and I believe it is—then it is a statement of revolutionary importance. It means that there is a whole area of our being that we do not understand.

Let me try to clarify what I mean with an example. In the nineteenth century, many doctors were fascinated by the phenomenon of hypnosis, although many of them regarded it as a fraud. One of them was a young schoolteacher named Alfred Russel Wallace, who would later be the co-discoverer of the theory of evolution. As a young teacher, Wallace discovered that a number of his pupils were excellent hypnotic subjects. One boy was so good that he would actually share Wallace's sensations. If Wallace pinched his own arm, the boy would start and rub his own arm. If Wallace tasted sugar, the boy smiled and licked his lips. If Wallace tasted salt, the boy grimaced. Later, the same experiments were repeated by one of the founder members of the Society for Psychical Research, William Barrett. Now, according to modern psychology, hypnosis is merely a matter of "suggestion." You suggest to someone that they are tired, and they yawn. You suggest that they are going into a trance, and they go into a trance. In other words, they "do it themselves." But the experiments of Wallace and Barrett seemed to prove that this is not entirely true. They proved that hypnosis involves some kind of telepathy.

Other hypnotists did experiments in which they persuaded good hypnotic subjects to carry out their orders without actually speaking. One of them could blindfold a girl when she was under hypnosis and then give her telepathic orders—such as go to the next room, take the box of matches off the mantle shelf, and bring it back here to me.

One famous psychologist, Pierre Janet, was actually able to place a woman under hypnosis from the other side of Le Havre and order her to perform various actions.

In other words, Wallace, Barrett, and Janet were exercising psychic powers and were proving beyond doubt that these existed. Yet, although they were scientists who placed their results on record, they made no impression whatever on other scientists. Their colleagues felt that they preferred simple, down-to-earth physical explanations and totally ignored their discoveries.

Toward the end of the last century, when these things took place, this made no real difference. Science was man's attempt to "rise on stepping stones of his dead selves to higher things." Its discoveries would improve society until there was no more poverty, injustice, or misery. H. G. Wells wrote books with titles like *A Modern Utopia* or *Men Like Gods* to express this vision of science.

The problem was that science came to feel that it could explain everything in purely material terms. Life was simply a product of chance. Man did not possess a "spirit" or a soul; personality could not be explained purely in terms of control units of the brain and the way that they were influenced by experience. Man is shaped by his experience in exactly the same way that a weathered rock is shaped by the wind and the rain. Communism announced that religion was the "opium of the people," and what all human beings needed to make them happy was material wealth. The democratic countries believed in exactly the same thing, except that they also believed in allowing people to vote for their own government.

The result is the modern world, as we know it—brutal, materialistic, obsessed by success. Yet our culture is strangely pessimistic; for more than a century now, fashionable plays and novels have been based on the assumption that human beings are weak and helpless and that our destiny is to be defeated and destroyed. Samuel Beckett was given a Nobel Prize for assuring us that life was meaningless.

It is not difficult to trace a connection between this pessimism and the "reductionism" of science. In the twentieth century, the average man has had to learn to cope with complications that would have given Dante or Shakespeare a nervous breakdown. Yet, in spite of all his efforts, science assures him that life is meaningless.

Now it can be seen why I am so enthusiastic about Bob Cracknell. He knows from experience that man possesses a "spirit," and that the human mind is not simply a product of the human body.

In fact, all that I have just said here has been said more simply and briefly in Bob Cracknell's parable of the two frogs, which follows this introduction. Bob is the frog who has been blown down to the bottom of the well and whose comments about the life "up there" completely bewilder the frog that has spent his life at the bottom of the well.

But there is one minor respect in which Bob's parable does not conform to actuality. The truth is that most frogs that live at the bottom of wells have a strange longing for something they do not understand. In their dreams, they see a land with trees and flowers. Modern society is full of people who, in the last analysis, feel that they do not "belong" to this apparently solid common material world. They feel that there "must" be some way of living that gives them more satisfaction than the world in which they find themselves.

In my first book, I called such people "outsiders." Most of them have no idea why they feel vaguely dissatisfied with their lives and why they would like some more purposeful form of existence. They only know that going to work and coming home five times a week, and watching television all weekend, leaves them oddly dissatisfied.

In fact, we are all vaguely aware that we possess faculties we never use, senses that we do not understand. I am "ESP thick," I am certain that if I had been sitting beside Scrooge on Christmas Eve, I would not have seen Marley's ghost. Yet, even I know that extrasensory perception exists. Once on a trip to Scotland, I found myself plunged into a strange depression. Seeing that my wife also looked depressed, I asked her if she felt all right, and she admitted that she had an agonizing toothache. Her toothache and my depression lasted throughout the whole of the following day, a Sunday. Finally, in a little coastal town, she went to see a dentist. And as I was walking around the town with my little daughter, my depression abruptly lifted, and I said: "Your Mummy has had her tooth out." I proved to be correct—she had had it pulled out at that exact moment.

Every married couple has had the experience of suddenly knowing what the other one is thinking or feeling, or both starting to say the same thing at exactly the same moment. Human beings are naturally telepathic, but we need to be in the right state of mind in order to notice it. My dogs are certainly telepathic. They know exactly when I am coming upstairs from my desk to take them for a walk and when I am merely coming up to make myself a cup of tea. The wife of the Scottish poet Hugh McDiarmid told me that she always knew when he was coming back from a long journey, because their dog went and sat at the end of the lane and waited for him about two days before he returned . On one occasion, when his plans changed unexpectedly, the dog even knew when he was coming home before he did.

So in fact, we are not really separate individuals living in little airtight containers. We are much more like fish swimming in the same sea, and we can feel the pressure from other fish—even when they swim twenty yards away from us.

All primitive people seem to know this. In Canada, when a Montagnais Indian wants to communicate with a distant relative, he goes into a hut in the forest, places himself in a state of perfect calm, and then somehow transmits his thoughts to the relative. Jean Cocteau tells a story of a professor friend of his who asked an Indian woman: "Why do you talk to a tree?" The woman replied: "Because I am poor. If I were rich, I would use a telephone."

Now it may seem that becoming "ESP thick" is the price that we have paid for our modern civilization, with its trains, airplanes, and television sets. Yet, that is plainly not true. There are hundreds—probably thousands—of psychics like Bob Cracknell who can suddenly "know" things that the rest of us do not know.

As Bob has grown older, I have noticed a change in him. He has become gentler, more thoughtful. Eight years ago, after a turbulent and often dramatic life, he decided to retire to Cyprus and to spend his remaining years relaxing and enjoying the sunshine. But he is too much of a man of action to relax in the sun, and occasional telephone calls made me aware that he was as busy as ever and planning just as many projects. Nevertheless, few of his neighbors were aware that he was a famous psychic.

I am afraid that I was partly responsible for destroying his anonymity. I wrote an article in the *Daily Mail* describing the Janie Shepherd case. Within days, Bob was receiving phone calls from newspapers and television producers. Once again he became involved in the world of psychic detection.

The most important product of this emergence from retirement is the book you now hold in your hands. Many mediums and clairvoyants have written books about what it means to be psychic, but no one has explained with such simplicity and clarity how easy it is to make use of our psychic faculties. But, above all, he makes it clear why we should make use of them. Psychics are not people who see ghosts and communicate with the dead. They are simply people who are in possession of all their faculties—or, at least, more of them than the rest of us. We all feel it is important to be able to see the colors of the sunset, smell the scent of flowers, hear the sound of birds. We use our senses to "know" things outside us. The psychic is simply the person who possesses a kind of extra sense—or perhaps an extension of the other senses—that enables him to "know" more than the rest of us. Bob Cracknell's book not only explains this, but it also describes how it can be developed.

I feel proud of the small part I have played in bringing it into the world.

—Colin Wilson
Author of *Alien Dawn* and *The Outsider*

Prologue

Once upon a time, there were two frogs, unaware of each other. One lived at the bottom of a deep well. The other lived in the surrounding areas above the well. One day there was a tremendous storm that caused much flooding and a wind that blew down the trees. As a result of its strength, the current of the rainwater caught up the frog who had lived all its life on the land and carried it down to the bottom of the well.

After a short while, having adjusted to its new environment, the land frog came face-to-face with the frog that had lived all its life in the well. "Where did you come from?" asked the well frog.

"I came from up there. That was my home," replied the land frog.

"Yes, but where did you come from?" repeated the well frog.

"I came from up there," said the second frog.

"What's 'up there'?" asked the well frog.

"Oh, it's a big area, with trees and bushes and flowers."

"What are 'trees'?" asked the well frog. "What are 'flowers'?"

The land frog thought for a moment. "A tree is an enormous thing. It grows from the ground, all the way up—almost to the sky. . . . It has lots of big branches . . ."

"Hold on a minute," said the well frog impatiently. "What are you on about? It's got all these 'branches' and grows from the 'ground.' What's ground? Look around you. See what I have here. I have water and moss. . . . But, 'trees, flowers, branches and ground' I don't understand."

"Oh, yes—and there are snakes," said the land frog excitedly. "You have to be careful of snakes because they're very partial to us frogs, and if they get the chance, they'll eat us."

"What *are* you on about?" asked the well frog.

"Well, a snake is a creature—long, black and green. . . ."

"Just a moment," interrupted the well frog. "I don't care where you come from, or what your game is, but don't come down here disturbing me, telling me all this rubbish. It's a load of nonsense! Go away!"

chapter 1 The Psychic Reality

My name is Robert Cracknell. I have risen to the top of my profession. I am a psychic whose abilities have been forged in the harsh fires of a cynical, fearful, stereotypical world. I state that I am a psychic in the same way as another person might say: "I am an electrician," or "I am a baker."

Unlike other professions, my apprenticeship has taken place over a period of thirty-five years, where I have continuously and steadfastly sought to improve my abilities—and will continue to do so until it is my time to leave this third-dimensional existence.

I am not a guru, and I refuse to be labeled as such. I lay before you in this book the practical experience and wisdom I have gained in my life, often through painful personal experiences of loneliness, isolation, and rejection.

If you choose to label me as a teacher, then that is your choice. My purpose in writing this book is to pass on what I know, the knowledge that is my psychic reality at my present level of awareness. I hope you will find it to be of benefit.

My aim is to help facilitate an easier passage for those that come after me than the rites of passage I had to endure. Today, we live in a much more enlightened world than the one in which I was raised. Many people now say we are at the dawning of a golden age of spiritual awareness and scientific and psychic discovery, where even the statement "we are all psychic" sounds rather passé and tame.

Believe me, I am not unique. Each and every one of you has the same latent psychic ability within you that I do, which for the most part, is probably lying dormant but can easily be enhanced and refined until your inherent psychic ability can become of sound, practical benefit to you in your life. It can be incorporated into the "normal" five operational senses and can be utilized as a proper sense—your sixth sense. In time, it will become your most valuable sense, enabling the pursuit of wisdom, energy, serenity, and truth, according to your present level of awareness.

Developing your inherent psychic ability will give you an edge in your business life, your personal life and your social life. It will give you a far deeper understanding of each and every interpersonal relationship you will encounter in your life. This will not always be a bed of roses—there will be some thorns—but as life becomes more complex and frenetic, you will be better able to control your life, enrich your relationships, and develop into a fuller, more rounded, more confident, and happier individual in the new age that awaits us all.

Look around and you will find many people searching to find greater meaning to their present existence. Many people realize or sense that their lives are incomplete, that they are not in touch with others and certainly are not in touch with themselves. People all over the world are seeking awareness, and I hope that within the words and the spirit of this book, they will find it.

Time and time again, in all fields of human endeavor, we encounter the word "truth." Perhaps the most famous confrontation was that purported to have taken place between Pontius Pilate and Jesus in the Bible, when during his trial, Jesus said: "I have come into the world to bear witness to the truth. Everyone who is of the truth hears my voice."

Pilate retorted: "What is truth?"

Perhaps both men knew that truth as an immutable, fixed, universal reference point cannot exist.

An individual's perception of truth is determined by the level of awareness at a particular moment in time. Now. Now is the key word. Now is now. Now has gone. It is now again. At any point, your understanding, your awareness can alter.

Absolute truths and relative truths also relate to the world of physics and science. Those scientific facts and truths that were enshrined hundreds of years ago are now, one by one, being revised, overturned, or rejected as science's present level of awareness continues to advance.

It is no different in the world of the paranormal and the psychic. My heightened state of sensory awareness in my youth was labeled as some sort of nervous breakdown, but scientific awareness has progressed to the point where developed psychic ability is becoming accepted.

My truth, what I term the psychic reality, is that we stand on the threshold of a tremendous leap forward in our understanding of ourselves and the world we live in, where the psychic and the scientist could and should work hand in hand with each other to push the boundaries of known knowledge to their very limit, to the tangible benefit of all mankind.

But we certainly have barriers to overcome before we can truly set out on a quest for awareness, truth, and knowledge. These barriers, some of which are quite fundamental, exist in both the scientific world and the paranormal world, and they represent serious obstacles to mankind's future progress in both disciplines.

Most people when they hear the word "psychic," immediately associate it with clairvoyance, tarot reading, and fortune-tellers: in other words, people who claim to be able to predict the future—your future. It is interesting to note that even the media have a kind of sneering acceptance of what we might put under the catch-all umbrella of the "New Age"—astrology, extraterrestrial activity, reincarnation, the supernatural, ghosts and demons, spiritualism, the unexplained, mind, body and spirit, the latest fads, isms, and downright mumbo jumbo psychobabble and psychic babble.

During my meditative sabbatical, I have observed the rise of this New Age movement. I have attended lectures and seminars, read newspaper and magazine articles, and watched various performances on television concerning different aspects of the New Age. I have even personally questioned those who advertise themselves and sell their wares to a ready and, I am sorry to say, gullible collection of individuals who are plainly searching for some sort of personal enlightenment, but are quite frankly being ripped off.

I recently attended a Mind, Body and Spirit exhibition and left in disgust after a few minutes. The predominant impression I was left with was that most of the exhibitors were on "get-rich-quick" schemes and had such a shallow or nonexistent understanding of the psychic faculty that in another age they would have been denounced as fakes and charlatans and run out of town.

Nowadays, we can be far too civilized and polite to challenge a purveyor of some New Age idea or movement concerning the validity of whatever it is they are selling. And of course, unless the challenger is an experienced adept like myself, who not only knows what to look for but can tell in an instant whether that person is genuinely using their psychic faculty in an open, disclosed way, or is in fact dressing it up with pseudo-mystical props and nonsense to make it more mysterious and marketable, then the challenge can be daunting.

Worryingly, I have also detected that a group of people in the New Age movement are, for want of a better expression, psychobabble con men and women. They are the same type of professional profiteers who infiltrated and ultimately poisoned the Spiritualist movement around the turn of the century in both the United States and Europe. The same type of people illusionist Harry Houdini vowed to expose because he had the ability and experience to see right through the stage shows and the tricks of the trade that were being used in conning the public.

Unless we are very careful, the possible advances in the understanding of the psychic faculty could be buried by a cynical public and scientific backlash against the con men and the misguided amateurs exploiting and dabbling in this field of investigation.

The psychic reality is a discipline, a profession, that I have devoted the better part of my life to. I am not prepared to see charlatans and psychobabble merchants drag it back into a mire of misunderstanding, just when mankind has a real chance of making practical and revolutionary progress in this field.

If it becomes necessary to publicly challenge and expose the fakes, I will not shirk my responsibility. And I hope other psychic adepts share my views and will do likewise. I trust they will join me in finding a way to make the psychic reality a scientific reality, where the psychic and the scientist work together for the betterment of mankind.

7

I know that other psychic adepts feel the scientific community and the nature of parapsychological research has failed them. I myself have been publicly accused of being a crank until I forced a grudging public apology, but that was then and this is now. The future—a glorious future—awaits us if we are prepared to work together, to pool our psychic abilities and resources and wisdom, and to find a way of making that scientific breakthrough to the psychic reality.

Do we not have a responsibility to the new generation of psychics who sense the truth—the psychic reality—but are in danger of being led off into some sort of exploitative cul-de-sac? Are there not very real dangers in the psychic and third-dimensional world that the new generation is going to have to face—the prevalence of mind-altering drugs, the dangers of cloning, the growth of violent behavior, and the dabbling with the psychic reality without a proper appreciation of its power and any formal training?

Are we not allowing the new generation to play with fire when we, with the responsibility that comes with greater awareness, exhibit a petulant attitude because the scientists have failed us in our generation?

If the adepts do not become proactive in their discipline, then I suspect our epitaphs will make gloomy reading, and we will eventually be forgotten when the entire parapsychology field falls into disrepute because of the dabblings of the con artists and mumbo jumbo merchants.

Let me reiterate my understanding of the psychic reality at this point. We all have within us inherent psychic ability, which can be developed and enhanced until it is of practical benefit to us in our everyday lives.

This ability, whether it manifests itself in terms of clairvoyance, or healing, or counseling, is not given to us by an outside force, a spirit guide or guides, ghosts, gods, or magic crystals. And, for this reason, those who develop their psychic faculty cannot and must not shirk their personal responsibility.

People who have psychic impressions about others or about events must not absolve their personal responsibility for that psychic impression by saying that a spirit guide or some other external force passed it on to them—and that they were merely a go-between. This is at best misguided and at worst dishonest. These are individual psychic impressions, which we can all experience, and individuals must learn to accept them as their own. Then we will see true advancement of the understanding of the psychic faculty.

To be psychic—to be aware of the psychic faculty that lies dormant in each of you—is simply to be aware of what lies beyond the normal range of recognition as we understand it, within our third-dimensional state of existence.

Our physical consciousness is involved in what we understand and have been brought up to accept as normal. In other words, the third-dimensional state. Let us look at this.

A third-dimensional state indicates that there is also a first and second state, which science and logic provide—that is, height, depth, and width. Each state can be shown as separate and is recognized by our intellectual consciousness, by our involvement in the whole.

It is more than probable that there are more dimensions. How many? We don't know, because we cannot recognize that which does not exist within our immediate state of awareness. Working within the confines of our third-dimensional state, we are able to recognize, through our normal senses, the significance of our own makeup, and we are able to accept, without any deep analysis, the concept of duality: the duality of gender, of our existence (life and death) and most important, of

9

the conscious and subconscious. It is within this duality that we must search to find the awareness known as the psychic faculty, which, to the majority of us, has become hidden somewhere between these two states.

I would argue that the reason we, mainly in the Western Hemisphere, are unaware of this psychic faculty is because of our social conditioning since childhood.

Are we totally unaware? Ask yourself. Have you experienced feelings that you cannot identify? A feeling of a bad move perhaps? A feeling that you need to contact somebody? Or a feeling that something is about to happen? How many times *has* it happened?

We use the label "hunch"; we get a" hunch" about something or someone. I maintain that this is our basic psychic awareness operating. Because we don't understand this, we don't recognize it as such.

Societies that exist within our hemisphere, that are perhaps not what we would term "civilized," or perhaps that have not become enmeshed in materialism, use this faculty quite naturally. Take, for instance, the Aborigine. There are numerous recorded instances where a lone Aborigine, in the Australian Outback, would suddenly feel the necessity to return hundreds, sometimes thousands of miles, back to his tribe. They have the ability to sense when a natural disaster, such as a storm, is approaching. They are "in tune" because they do not have the burden of materialism. They are not concerned with materialism; only with their day-to-day living and their need for basic nourishment. Their senses are sharp. They are in tune with their environment.

We are not in tune with the natural environment; we are in tune with a chaotic man-made environment—an environment that dictates to us—and the pressure of earning a living and coping with life has taken away our ability to survive in a hostile world without the material necessities.

I used the term "hostile" deliberately. The majority of people would not be aware of this hostile environment. It prevents them from becoming aware of what they really are. They are aware only of their immediate material needs and of their physical state of existence.

Over the last ten years, however, we have begun to revolt against the conditioning that has been forced upon us. Many organizations, societies, groups, and individuals have begun searching for peace and understanding in order to control their own destiny. And many people practice meditation, which at its simplest level gives the opportunity to withdraw within oneself away from the external pressures of everyday living. Is it because of fear, that inherent fear that is uppermost in the minds of the majority? A fear of the unknown? A fear that has separated us from ways that we would term primitive, that has widened the gulf between the subconscious and the conscious?

Virtually all of us have been subjected, from a very early age, to religious teaching of some description or other. One of the first questions on any official form is invariably: "What is your religion?" Religion has been necessary for us, as a society, to be able to compete against this fear. From our very early beginnings, as children, a wall has been built up between that state of awareness that we accept as reality and that which lies deeply within our subconscious. Because we do not understand it, we fear it.

Regardless of your intelligence, your consciousness, at this moment of time, I would suggest that this wall that has been built, brick by brick, from your childhood, has become solid. It is this that prevents you from being able to cross through to that "nothing" state that exists within your own self.

Having made my opening statement quite clearly, that I am psychic—but that I am no different from any other person—the obvious challenge for me is to prove it. Initially, I can only express myself using words, words that can be confusing and, according to each individual's awareness, conflicting.

I would ask, therefore, that you bear with me. Let us try to avoid being pedantic. Let us accept that initially the use of words is the only possible avenue to reaching an understanding.

Truth does not exist. It is determined by your level of awareness now, which is constantly fluctuating. "Now" is the key word. Now is now. Now has gone. It is now again. At any point, your understanding, your awareness, can alter. Slowly, step by step, we must begin to break down this wall that has been built for us and by us. We must overcome preconceived ideas. We can stop now and argue according to our personal beliefs, and everyone's point of view is important. Our beliefs differ. But arguing or discussing is not achieving a universal understanding. Although we may agree in many instances, we have to compromise. This, I would argue, is not the way.

But first, let us try to weaken this wall that exists. As I have stated, we have all been subjected to some form of religious instruction. We are aware of the teachings the Bible purports to give us. However, the Bible itself is made up of words, the only medium available to us. As we grow older, many of us begin to analyze these words and this so-called truth.

We begin to question the validity of statements that are made, because they do not make sense to us. But what do we put in their place? Nothing—it is already there, hidden behind the brick wall of preconception. So let us knock down the wall. First, by loosening the very cornerstone, religion.

Genesis. The beginning. The first book of the Bible. Perhaps, in our present climate, we don't treat it with the respect that it truly deserves. Many cults, particularly those that become involved in magic, black or white, base their whole philosophy on its content. They have accepted the importance of Genesis. So I think it is important that we should look at it.

The teaching of Genesis is this: In the beginning was the word and the word was God. And the face of God moved upon the earth, which was dark and without form. Now, straight away, I am going to upset many people by bringing God into the equation. However, I do not wish to offend those whose belief is firmly entrenched in God. I hope, at a later stage, to be able to suggest possible alternatives to what we know as God.

But let us go back to that opening statement: the earth was dark and without form. In the beginning was God. We cannot imagine anything "without form," so let us try a very basic experiment. Close your eyes and concentrate on nothing. What do you visualize? If you say nothing, it seems to be a contradiction, as you are visualizing something.

If you break the "nothing" down into two syllables—that is, " no" and "thing"—perhaps we can then take our first step. In the beginning, there was "no-thing." This no-thing is even more confusing than the term nothing. There has to be something for us to create the image, so let's start again.

With your eyes closed, and concentrating upon no-thing, create in your mind a circle. What do you see? Something. A circle. What is in the center of the circle? That which existed *before* you created the circle. Nothing. No-thing. Which is the reality? Which is your reality now? Is it your third-dimensional physical state? Is that reality? Is the circle that you have created in order to recognize that "no-thing" the reality?

13

Can we perhaps, for argument's sake, look at the circle and relate it to our physical state. This is us; this is something solid, something recognizable. That which is within, exists without the illusionary circle. The reality must be what was.

Therefore, if in the beginning (a rather vague word to describe the original state of existence) there was no-thing and if this no-thing is what has become the cornerstone of the wall known as God, *you* are God. Not part of God. You are God. Visualize, on a wider scale, a blank wall. Wherever you create that circle, you have a recognition point. But you can draw that circle at any point on that blank space. If the blank space also represents existence, we have a problem, because all these circles that have been created and have been dotted all over the place seem to have no connection whatsoever. Why is that? What *is* normal? What is "psychologically correct"? Nothing. There is no normality.

For a society to form, to live together and to exist, there must be "norm." All psychologists work upon the basis of normality. All those who are said to suffer from psychological disorders are viewed as not "normal." The psychologist's role is to create or to accept whatever has been presented to him—a level of normality. In the treatment of those who have what is termed psychological disorders, their only objective is to attempt to get the individual to conform, as near as possible, to the level of normality that has been dictated.

It is odd that not one of us, including the psychologist who is attempting to restore this "normality" to individuals, is able to conform completely with this level.

I am not scientifically trained, nor am I inclined to attempt to argue or explain the origins of the Earth. It is not my intention to side either with those who believe totally in the Earth's creation by God, or with those who would argue that it came as a result of evolution, from a single cell, as a result of a cosmic explosion. I don't know. It doesn't matter.

The only important thing to accept is that in the original state of existence, there *was*, there *is*, and, it is logical to argue, there *will be*.

Genesis jumps about quite a lot. We all know that the concept of God creating something within seven days is symbolic. But, nonetheless, existence of the physical state began. Even the evolutionists' theory—that we evolved from apes—is equally correct. However, from what source did apes evolve? It becomes more and more complex. There is no need to get lost in this morass, though, so let us simply accept that *we are*.

Genesis goes on to say that, having created everything, God looked back and was happy with what had been achieved and so decreed a day of rest.

Fine, but then God decided to create an image "unto himself." This is totally confusing. If he created an image of himself, he would create nothing—no-thing. According to Genesis, he created Adam. Let us follow the least line of resistance, just for the sake of taking a further step on this long journey to achieving awareness. Let us accept that in the beginning evolution took place, and as a result of evolution, a species called Adam evolved. An animal, a species.

Let us go along this road without making detours, or allowing our intellect to confuse the issue. Adam was androgynous. Adam was a species that was both male and female. Here, Genesis begins to make sense. All that existed was peace and harmony. Nature controlled the balance. There was no intellect, and there was no understanding, but there *was* awareness.

Each creature, each tree, was aware of its existence, simply by "being." Genesis calls this the Garden of

Eden. Perfection. There was nothing other than the state of being. The continuous cycle of life and death and evolution of every species was natural. An animal that ate another animal for food was only eating to survive. It had created a continuous circle. Two animals fighting did not constitute a war.

So, into this situation came the androgynous creature "Adam." As a result of evolution, this androgynous creature began to develop and ultimately divided, from the one state evolution created it into two. The androgynous creature became male and female. In spite of this, the creature remained unaware, and perfect, as symbolized by the imagery of the Garden of Eden.

The two parts of the creature Adam would have continued to live totally unaware of one another, if not for a recognition of a similarity between them. Genesis puts its finger on the truth, symbolized by the serpent approaching Eve and saying: "There is a tree there with some apples on it." According to the teachings, God had said: "You can have anything you want. . . . But don't touch the apples. Leave the apples alone."

You all know the story, of course. Eve said to Adam: "Here, have a bite of this." Adam objected, saying he wasn't allowed to. But Eve persisted and so he had a bite.

The most important thing that Genesis teaches us is that as a result of this, one day God came visiting and Adam ran away. And God asked him why he was hiding from him. To quote from Genesis, Adam replied: "Because I am naked." Here, I believe, is the nub of the whole question. We find an awareness. God asked: "Who told you, you were naked?"

What had happened? Evolution had continued to a point where the two species, the two opposites of the original Adam, male and female, began to recognize and allow themselves to understand the meaning of sexuality—and possibly introduced, for the very first time, an awareness of duality, of male and female. This was symbolized by God saying to Adam: "Who told you, you were naked?"

Man became aware of itself. This duality introduced a more subtle awareness of its environment and altered what existed. We could stop right now and argue the merits of what I have just proposed, but I am sure we would succeed in offending every priest in existence.

I am not here to present to you what I believe is the truth. This is only the first lesson for us, to be able to accept something that guides us down the road to an awareness of ourselves—and "of being." In becoming aware of ourselves and our being, we become aware of all that is contained within the circle—everything. Not just being psychic, not just being able to have a better understanding of life, but becoming aware of this tremendous power that makes us what we are. To accept it is to accept that we have it within us. Our aim is to go one step further and to accept not only that it is within us but that *we are it.* That this power, this life force (call it what you will) is what we are. The physical state is simply a circle that encompasses what always has been. There is no limit to what we can achieve.

But, because we are part of this physical existence, we have to live and we have to survive. We must conform to the demands of society and not simply take up our begging bowls and escape to some distant island, contemplating our navels for the remainder of our days. It is impossible. It is equally impossible to overcome all our prejudices and our psychological makeup. Only then might we reach the state of perfection known as nirvana, bliss, perfect realization.

It is true that there are many individuals who have devoted their whole lives in an attempt to achieve that original state, the symbolic meaning of celibacy within the priesthood. How would you interpret this? Is it odd that such a strong established religious movement as Catholicism should adopt symbolically what all mystics who set out to attain perfection adopt? Celibacy. The mystic practices celibacy in an attempt to become that androgynous being, to enable the continuous flow of sexual energy to be contained within itself.

As we progress, we may have to step into minefields of philosophy and religious argument. I have simply attempted to eradicate the psychological grip that religion has gathered around us, without causing offence. By all means, retain your own beliefs—but if you wish to go one step further, then try to keep your minds open.

chapter 2 The First Step

I am not a salesman, offering "psychic awareness within seven days or your money back." I am simply an individual who wishes to pass on a message. What I am, so are you. What I have become, so can you.

It may seem odd that in the last chapter we talked about what everybody (whether they accept it or not) recognizes—the psychic. The psychic faculty, the psychic ability. And yet, we seem to have concentrated more on knocking down religious structures and arguing about philosophy.

What is the point of achieving psychic awareness? What does being a psychic mean? There are those who have achieved psychic awareness and use it in a practical sense and it is, in itself, considered a somewhat sterile talent. What good is it? What does it do?

So, you can predict what is going to happen. You can have a portent of events that may affect others. Surely, this in itself is of tremendous importance. For, make no mistake, there are those psychics among us who have been able to foresee events that have taken place.

If we are more aware and more tolerant of prediction, think of the possible results. A psychic is able to see a disaster that is about to happen. Fortunately, as a result of serious tests conducted by major universities of the world, we have become more open-minded. Psychics have been tested, over and over again, under scientific conditions, and are now being taken seriously. What one would call a "prediction" is simply an accurate portrayal of what is to happen. Numerous cases are logged where personal disasters have been averted by people being made aware of what is going to happen, enabling them to take positive steps to protect themselves against it.

Can a psychic predict the future? Strangely enough, no. The future is yet to come. The future is determined by what happens now. Some people subscribe to the theory that things are preordained, and that there is nothing we can do about it. I would argue against this.

The only certain thing in life is death. That is the only inevitable event that will affect each and every person. Even if, having become aware of your psychic faculty, you do not use it at a public level but only for yourself, you are able to foresee what will happen and, as a result of what you do now, you will be able to avoid the foreseeable by taking a positive action.

There are psychics who set themselves up and advertise their talents, inviting people to come along for a reading, where they will look into the crystal ball and tell you what is going to happen. The questions you want to ask are likely to be: Are my children going to be happy? Am I going to have enough money? Am I going to have a serious illness? Is anybody close to me going to die? These are questions the psychic can sometimes answer—and in many instances, what they say can come true.

What value does this type of psychic have? Not a lot, really, because the tendency is for people to rely upon what they say. If you negate any personal responsibility and say: "I have been told this is going to happen and there is nothing I can do to change things," this is dangerous. In my opinion, those psychics who leave such impressions in the minds of people cannot be considered responsible. They are doing no real good. You may argue, therefore, what is the point of achieving this psychic awareness?

Let us take other instances. I was known as "Britain's number one psychic detective." These are my credentials. I became involved in major police investigations. There is no necessity for me to relate these. My track record stands up to scrutiny. It is extremely impressive. Experiments conducted by the Oxford University Society for Psychical Research resulted in my achieving an 80 percent accuracy rating under controlled experiment conditions. You may read the results of these experiments, analyze them, and come to the conclusion: "Well, what is the value of that?"

But the proof is there. I am psychic and I am able to perceive certain events. And still you ask: "What value does this have?" It has value because I was able to give details about a murder, including the location of where the suspect lived.

Certain police forces are more willing than others to act upon the information given to them by the psychic. Others tend to "pooh-pooh" it, and when the psychic is proven to be correct, will often turn around and say: "Okay, so he was correct. But we established the facts and arrested the murderer as a result of straightforward normal police work and detection."

It really doesn't matter. There are far more important aspects of being psychic than this. And all that I have achieved as a result of being involved with police investigations, has been to accumulate a great deal of publicity and a large ego, which I hope I have, over the years, learned to control and use positively.

Let's look at the really important aspects. All parents, all mothers act on hunches. You will have heard many stories of a child being in one room and the mother in the next. Instantly, she has a feeling that something is wrong, and when she checks, she finds the child is in some kind of danger.

"Thank God I acted on my hunch," she says. But she didn't act on a hunch. She reacted to her psychic awareness. If that person were to truly develop this psychic awareness, think of the benefits—not for public consumption, but in a practical sense, in her everyday life.

Psychics become aware of the ability within themselves to project energy and power for the benefit of others. They become the unsung hero or heroine, perhaps, of the whole psychic scene, who, as a result of becoming aware, whether by accident or design, is able to put up his or her hand to touch other people and project this power, this energy, to have a beneficial effect on those who are suffering. This is fact.

These psychics have more importance than people such as myself going on national television or appearing in the national newspapers and saying: "I predict that the Yorkshire Ripper will commit one more murder and will be arrested on a certain day of the week; not by the CID, but by a policeman who will be checking cars." This happened. I did it. But, was I responsible? Did I cause the arrest of the Ripper? No. I was simply able to look ahead and "see" what was going to happen. I saw this future event and it was picked up by the national press. The publisher of my first book took great pleasure from it but that was all I did. It was nothing in comparison to those who can have a practical effect on people by bringing them peace, understanding, and healing. I consider that to be more important.

So, let us hope that together we can achieve something. Let us go down this pathway together, bearing in mind that words are the only vehicle I can use at this moment in time. Later on, as we progress, you may yourselves begin to understand the total inadequacy of words. Unfortunately, however, that can't happen straightaway.

If I may poach a famous expression: "The journey of a million miles begins with the first step." Let's take that step.

It is almost impossible for anyone who has been stimulated in any way to be able to switch off, mentally, and relax. They are still caught up in a maelstrom of feelings and emotions created by the stimulation, and it takes another jolt of action to their conscious mind to take over and deal with the new thought activity. To be angry, and have to listen to some well-meaning person telling you to relax, really doesn't help. The last thing you want to do is *not* be angry. It is too strong a feeling—and you need some form of alternative action to channel this energy.

For this book to succeed in helping you achieve your psychic potential, I have been deliberately provocative with what I have written so far—simply to cause a reaction.

So, how can you break from the reaction that you are experiencing, as a result of what you have read so far?

Meditation is the key! What is meditation? Simply a way to contemplate; to break through the immediate emotion of the present, and to relax. There are numerous ways of doing this, and it is not necessary to be concerned, to fear that you might lose control and enter into some form of trance.

As mentioned in the preface of this book, I have prepared a special cassette tape, with original, ethereal music, for those who might prefer to have some form of voice control.

Remember one important thing—the level of meditation which I am advocating has no dangers. You will *not* enter into any form of trance. Your subconscious mind will always be in control, ready and alert, should any external noise disturb you. Simply listening to soft, gentle music is as good a way as any of relaxing and meditating.

I would now advise that you continue reading to the end of the chapter and then prepare yourself to carry out the exercise.

Choose a time for your meditation when you are least likely to be disturbed. Have a relaxing bath or shower and eat a light, balanced meal so that your body is relaxed and not encumbered with digesting 'heavy' food. Take the telephone off the hook. If you prefer, play some soft and gentle, pastoral music that doesn't increase in volume. Relax. . . .

And as you begin to relax, once again become consciously aware of your body. Go from your feet, all the way along your legs, up through the body, to both arms, to the head. Concentrate on your physical body. Be aware of the fact that you are sitting there and that you are going over the various parts of your body.

Maybe you have an ache or a pain. Maybe your mind is active as a result of what you have heard or read. Maybe you want to discuss it more. Maybe it has caused some emotion in you and you cannot accept it. Just spend time concentrating upon it.

Now, feel the atmosphere around you. Feel it. What do you feel? Listen to the silence.

A simple exercise, to enable you to focus your mind—which also allows you to discipline your meditation—is to imagine that you have a hole, approximately one inch in diameter, at the top, dead-center, of your head; another at the center of your forehead; your throat;

heart; spleen; solar plexus; and midway between your sexual organ and your anus. To the true adept of meditation, these are known as the "chakras". For you—the beginner—they are simply "focal points". Focus on each point in turn and imagine a hole opening at each of those points. Having accomplished this, simply relax and allow your concentration to focus on the natural rhythm of your breathing.

This is all that is necessary for you to be able to escape from the immediate pressure of your physical body. If you are unable to achieve this, do not be concerned, just continue to relax and follow the natural rhythm of your breathing.

Now, you can be more aware of the silence. Be in that silence. Become aware of it. Feel how dense it is. There is nothing else. There is nothing to visualize. Just silence.

Come away from that silence now. Concentrate now on your eyes by simply being aware of your eyes. Nothing else. Only your eyes. Your normal everyday vision is natural. You may say I am looking at this or I am seeing that, but it takes no conscious effort to do it. You are simply using your eyes to visualize what is in front of them.

Now, while you are within this meditative state, with your eyes closed, continue to concentrate on them, and where your eyes are, substitute two holes.

Remain aware of those two holes where your eyes are and you will find that the concentration has created a slight edginess. Take a deep breath. Become extremely conscious of taking this breath, and as you exhale, feel your body begin to relax.

Feel the tension that has built up in that small act of concentrating on your eyes begin to flow away. Push it down to your feet. Push it out. And now, once again, allow the natural rhythm of your breathing to become your focal point, and as you begin to relax once again, take your concentration toward those two holes where your eyes were.

Now, look through those holes. You are looking through your eyes, not using them. Now stop. You cannot do this quickly. You have taken a small step but you will without question or doubt feel pressure around your forehead and your eyes.

Let us relieve this pressure. The pressure will not be intense—and a simple exercise will relieve it. Take your concentration to that imaginary hole at the top dead-center of your head and mentally close it down. A simple, but effective way is to envisage the hole and close it by forming the sign of a cross over it.

Do the same to all the other chakras, in turn.

Come down once again to the focal point of your breathing. Relax. Completely relax. Now spend a short time analyzing what you feel. You are not aware of your physical body, are you? Take your concentration to the top dead-center of your head and close down the chakras as you have been taught.

From the top dead-center of your head—close.

The forehead—close.

The throat—close.

The heart—close.

The spleen—close.

The solar plexus—close.

The kundalini—close.

Make an imaginary line from underneath your left foot, bring it up all around the left-hand side of your body, breathing in as you reach the top center of your head, continue with the line going down until it joins with the starting point underneath your right foot, breathing out.

Now, deliberately exhale. Just gently twitch your toes. Feel the sensation of your physical body. Become aware of it. You are back. To another state of awareness.

Do not be in a hurry to move about too quickly. Spend time now analyzing what you have experienced doing these exercises. Perhaps "analyze" is the wrong word. Remember. Remember those changes that have taken place. And, in your own time, open your eyes. Do not consciously look around you but feel the sensation around your eyes.

And, again, in your own good time, become alert and ready to resume your normal activity.

After a while, you should find it easy to relax and benefit from this simple form of meditation—and may feel the need to go a little deeper. For this, I strongly recommend voice control. As stated, there is a cassette tape, available by mail order, should you wish to avail yourself of this. Bearing in mind that the whole point of this book is to enable you to realize for yourself your own psychic ability, at the end of the book is a transcript of the tape. (You might have a sympathetic friend who will record the words for you.)

chapter 3 Understanding and Controlling the Chakras

There was once a priest from an orthodox religion who became somewhat dissatisfied with his state and began to question all that he had studied and learned. He began to disagree with his external God figure. He could embrace entirely the concept of an all-pervading power, but it conflicted with his orthodox training.

So, he set out to study more complex philosophies and religions, and his quest finally took him to an old guru, who lived alone in the Himalayas. Many people made pilgrimages to see the guru, as he was considered to be the master of spiritual knowledge.

The man spent years with this guru, absorbing all that the guru said and all that he did. The man observed the guru from every possible angle and came to revere the man totally. After some years, he felt that he had absorbed all that he could, but there was one thing that eluded him. So, one day, he went to the guru and said to him: "Master, you have taught many things. I have found peace within myself. I have overcome the confusion of my conventional training, and I now realize exactly who and what I am. But, you tell me, the whole basis of your teaching is that God is within.

"This doesn't differ from any other religion that I have studied, and yet you emphasize this above everything else. I think I have gone as far as I can and I must move on to pastures new—but, before I go, please show me this God within."

The guru looked at him and said: "Very well. Fetch me an acorn."

So, the man brought an acorn to the guru, and the guru then said: "Split the acorn in half."

The man was puzzled at this, but did as he was told.

The guru looked at him intently and said: "Show me the oak tree."

We are all aware of the five senses we use in our daily lives. We employ them naturally and we really don't place a great deal of emphasis upon them. They are part of our lives, like breathing.

Unless we are suffering some form of illness, or disease of the lungs, we are unaware of our breathing. It is a natural function. But, before we can enter within ourselves, we must understand not just the five senses, but we must try to reach that sixth sense—the sixth sense that is acknowledged, and that I term the psychic faculty.

We have already discussed the inadequacy of words. So now we must begin to try and picture, to imagine more fully, that which does not exist. And to do this I will introduce you to what the adept acknowledges as chakras, or psychic senses.

To the fully trained practitioner, there are many chakras. But, for the purpose of our beginning, we will concentrate on seven.

The top dead-center of your head is your first chakra. The center of the forehead is your second. The center of your throat is your third. The area of your heart is the fourth. The area within the middle of your rib cage, roughly located around the spleen, is your fifth. The solar plexus is your sixth. And the seventh is at a point midway between the sexual organ and the anus.

These are the seven points. As an exercise, try to imagine that these points are holes. The top dead-center of the head is the chakra that is used for expansion of consciousness. The center of the forehead, often used and sometimes known as the third eye, is symbolically associated with clairvoyance—clear vision. The center of the throat is used in conjunction with clairaudience—clear hearing. The center of the heart is the whole of our functioning. The center of the spleen is used for purification of the rest of the chakras. The center of the solar plexus, the most vulnerable chakra of all, is the center of all vibrations. It is the chakra that we must first concentrate on and, more important, the one that we must be able to control and keep closed down. The center situated between the sexual organ and the anus is a chakra known as the kundalini. It is unlikely you will be able to concentrate on it too much, in the sense that it is very seldom used by those of us who live in the Western societies. Only the true adept, a yogi from the East, can concentrate on this. It is necessary to explain this because at all times we must be aware of it and be able to use it. For it is considered to be the very essence of life force. It is the center of all sexual energy and to be able to uncoil it and use it, entirely for spiritual purposes, one must practice complete and absolute celibacy. There must be no waste of seminal fluid. It takes years and years of practice and determination to be able to uncoil the kundalini and to enter into what the true yogi calls complete awareness.

As we progress, we will naturally concentrate on each chakra in turn.

The first exercise is to relax as much as possible. Sit down at a time when you know you are unlikely to be disturbed. Initially, this will be difficult because our first awareness is of our conscious body. Our second awareness is that we have closed our eyes and we are attempting to relax. ~~To a certain extent, it becomes almost impossible to relax simply by concentrating on this word.~~

As you sit down comfortably, with your eyes closed and in a relaxed frame of mind, concentrate first on what you are doing automatically but of which you are unaware. Concentrate on your breathing—on the natural gentle rhythm. As you concentrate, you may be aware that your breathing is a little fast or a little harsh. Spend time just concentrating on it, and at all times become involved with the gentle rhythm of your breathing.

After a while (once you are feeling relaxed and there is nothing to disturb you), take your concentration to the top dead-center of your head. Imagine there is a ~~hole~~. [VIOLET] Concentrate on this until your imagination has been able to create the ~~hole~~. Then, bring ~~down~~ your concentration to the center of your forehead. Again, create a ~~hole~~ at this [INDIGO] point. Continue in the same way, down to the center of [DARK DENIM] the throat, to the center of the heart, to the center of the [BLUE] [PINK] [GREEN] [YELLOW] ~~spleen~~, to the center of the solar plexus, and to the center [ORANGE] of the kundalini. [RED]

Do not create a hole at the kundalini. Just concentrate on that point, and then come back up again, to the center of the solar plexus. [ORANGE] Spend some time on this center. Divert your whole concentration to it. You may feel a slight uneasiness. Do not concern yourself but concentrate on it. For this is the first one that we must understand and control.

Bring your concentration up now, through to the [YELLOW] [PINK-GREEN] [BLUE] [INDIGO] [VIOLET] spleen, the heart, the throat, and the top dead-center of your head. Remain there for a short period of time, just concentrating on the top dead-center of your head. Any uneasiness that you may have felt, as a result of concentrating on the solar plexus, should disappear. There is no guarantee that you will experience any of these sensations, but spend a short period of time and try to analyze what you are feeling and experiencing.

The first thing you should experience is a calm sensation. You have now opened your chakras. You have opened your psychic senses and you can remain in this state for a short period of time. But having done so, you cannot just open your eyes and concern yourself once again with your everyday happenings. For, having opened your chakras, you must now close them again.

Beginning at the top dead-center of your head, concentrate on the imaginary hole you have created and put a cross on the top of the hole. It may help to be able to effect this by simply visualizing the sign of the cross—the four points covering the hole that you have created.

Then, to the center of the forehead. Follow the same procedure, to the throat, to the heart, to the spleen, to the solar plexus, and to the kundalini. Picture yourself externally as you are sitting and relaxing. Concentrate at the bottom, the underneath of your left foot. Slowly, draw an imaginary line from underneath your left foot, up around the left-hand side of your body, to the center of the top of your head.

While doing this, take a deep breath in. Having reached the top-center of your head, continue with the line down the right-hand side of your body, underneath your right foot, and joining with the beginning of the imaginary line of your left foot. This time breathe out as you go down. You have, in effect, drawn an imaginary circle all the way around your body.

You have now closed your chakras and enclosed what we will call the aura—the outside physical emanations of our physical body. Relax for a short period of time, then open your eyes gradually. That is all.

Practice this once a day, if it is possible. If you are a member of a group, this will become part of your everyday meditation and learning to reach the psychic faculty. Having completed this exercise, there is no necessity (in fact, I question whether you would want to do so) to get up and busy yourself with something physical. Try and analyze what you have experienced. Have you been able to follow, or has your mind been too active—therefore denying you the opportunity? Have you rejected it as a load of nonsense? Analyze. Do not dismiss it as nonsense. It is the first step and a vital one. But, whatever you have experienced, accept.

The first and most important chakra, and the most vulnerable, is the one situated in the solar plexus. It is the center of vibrations. It is where you receive all the nasty vibrations. How many of you can now understand? You have a terrible feeling within this area. Something is about to happen?

As a child, when you were called in to see your parents, you knew you had done something wrong and a punishment was due. You felt it in your stomach—your solar plexus.

It has become a common expression: "I have a terrible feeling in the pit of my stomach. Something nasty is about to happen." This is the lowest of all chakras and it is one that is open in all people, without them being aware of it. It is the one that can prevent you from getting a clear picture, and it is the one that we must, from "day one," begin to control.

When you get an uneasy feeling there, bring it up to the center of the forehead to try and "visualize," to break through the emotion that is causing this feeling within your stomach. Try to be able to "see" clearly.

As I have said, all people operate subconsciously with the chakra of their solar plexus. It is the lowest and it is one that is totally unnecessary; but, now you are aware of it, we are able to control it and block it out. We don't want to know. You may be sitting with a group of people and feel something emanating from another person. It is coming from them and it is coming into you through your solar plexus. You can't analyze it yet, but as you become more and more adept, you will be able to bring it up to the center of your forehead and translate it, to understand what it is that this person is pumping out—without being conscious of it.

In essence, the psychic receives these vibrations via the solar plexus and, without any training whatsoever, can quickly feel something untoward. Many times, he or she can pinpoint the reason for this uneasiness. It may be something affecting a member of the family, an unpleasant event that is about to take place, or some bad news. How many of you have experienced this psychic reception and yet not accepted it as such?

As a result of what I have just told you, you should now be able to recognize this reception. I hope you are able to say, "Yes, I have experienced it!"

How many of you have been invited to somebody's home, or maybe gone 'round to a friend's house for a meal? You've been looking forward to it. You arrive with your partner. Your host opens the door and says: "Hi! How are you? Er . . . sorry, we're running a little late. Come in, sit down, and have a drink." You are given a drink and told that your host's partner is just getting ready and they'll join you shortly.

As the host leaves the room and you are left sitting there, how many times have you felt uneasy? You look across to your partner. It is as if there has been one hell of an argument there in that house, and you can almost "feel" it. Have you ever thought that all you are doing is absorbing the vibrations that remain extremely strong, because the argument has only recently finished? A swirling of vibrations has remained in the room. All the energy that has been spent in arguing has yet to dissipate. Consequently, you are feeling this discomfort and you are able to interpret it correctly.

I am sure the vast majority of you have experienced an event of this nature. You are psychic but you are unaware of it. Later on, with training, not only will you understand they have had an argument but you will not allow it to affect you. The discomfort that is hitting your solar plexus will not affect you. You will be able to look at it objectively and recognize what has taken place and achieve a greater understanding of the whole situation. But, initially, you will be operating at a very crude level and it will cause you uneasiness.

Always try to define the vibrations that swirl around—this tremendous burst of energy. How many times have you expressed anger, against your partner, your children, or even against yourself? This anger builds up and you can't rid yourself of it. It is all around you. The whole room becomes filled with a swirl of emotion, because there is nowhere for it to go. It remains—and it affects you.

How many times have you suffered from a terrible headache, as a result of a violent argument with your partner? The tension stays with you. There is nowhere for it to go. So, go out to visit somebody. Let the tension go—relax.

Another example. Somebody calls round for a coffee. You open the door to them. Instantly you feel uneasy. You are picking something up from this person—and it is hitting your solar plexus. But it is not instantly recognizable. It is affecting them and it is also affecting you because you are receiving it at the bottom level. You are aware of it, and it is causing you some discomfort. You might not pick up the symptoms, but you take on their tension.

I have often visited locations where a murder has taken place. The police seek help on many occasions from people such as myself. They have no answers or clues as to what took place. They only know that somebody was brutally murdered in the room. The more violent the event, the greater the energy field that is left in that location, and the longer it takes to dissipate.

Any one of you, without knowing that a violent murder had taken place in that room some hours before, would walk in and experience a terrible feeling of uneasiness. Of this, I am sure.

On the occasions when I was called in, I had to remain objective, not let the violence and the resultant energy hit my solar plexus and disturb me. I had to get above it; to try and get a clear picture of what physically happened in that room. In the majority of cases, I was able to describe what had actually taken place there. The police, as a result of their investigations, had pieced together events and had come to the same conclusion. There always remains an element of doubt, but to be able to feel the event and describe it can be of great value.

Many psychics are known by another term—medium: one who is able to communicate with the dead. And this instantly conjures up the subject of ghosts and spirits. We will discuss this later at greater length. But, I will make a qualification straightaway by saying that I do accept this phenomenon. I accept it totally, and the term "ghost" will be defined later in some detail.

Most cases of paranormal activity are as a result of a disturbed mind, or some event (such as a murder) that has been out of the ordinary. Therefore, the energy released is so great that nothing seems to be able to disperse it. But, what did take place there? Whereas the medium can sense the atmosphere and say (for example): "I see a figure. . . . There was suicide, something violent here," this might not necessarily mean that the ghost *is* the actual person who died, but it is locked within this swirling mass of vibration and cannot escape. It remains at the scene.

In that simple statement it seems as though one would dismiss completely the idea of spirits and ghosts, and that people who die in strange or violent circumstances are able to communicate with us. I do not dismiss it. At one time, I myself found myself operating in the only avenue that was open to me at this time, which was Spiritualism.

I became known as the most controversial medium on "the circuit," because I argued against the principals of Spiritualism. I also argued against the principles of mediumship. A medium is simply a person who is able to communicate with the departed, the dead. Mediums can deny responsibility for their actions by claiming that they are controlled by the spirit of a dead person, that the information they are transmitting is being received from this vague "spiritual world." They are "guided" and, therefore, anything they say absolves them from responsibility because they haven't said it. The spirit has. I am totally against this personal concept, but at the same time will not condemn, out of hand, all Spiritualist mediums. The majority of them are sincere and excellent psychics but they have yet to overcome that psychological barrier of taking responsibility for themselves and admitting that they are psychic, and because of this can see and feel certain things.

Is there life after death? I believe there is a continuation of existence. In cases where I myself have been able to describe people that have died in accurate detail, I do not necessarily accept that those people still exist in the way I have described them, relative to their physical state. It is the only way they can be recognized. Therefore, this is a matter that is open for discussion and your own interpretation, as you develop. I would simply say that if we can accept the statement, "I am, I was, I will be," there are grounds for believing in the continuation of existence. There seems to be little point in going through the trials and tribulations of a physical state on earth simply to wake up "on the other side" and spend the rest of eternity communicating on a very emotional level with those in a physical state of existence. To me, this is not on, and it doesn't mean anything. I don't know the answers to give you.

I believe in a continuation of life after death. I believe it strongly. I do not know what state of existence that will be until such time as I am there, but I can see no value in trying to communicate information back, through a foggy mist, for some people to interpret.

Let us try another simple exercise. Think of a person you once knew who is now dead. Concentrate on that person. Picture them in your mind. What are they doing? You can picture them in any environment whatsoever, and while you are picturing them, they exist. They exist because they were. They might be laughing or crying. Your mind can create whatever you want to see.

But I would rather concentrate on what you do not know and on what your subconscious mind will present to you, for you to be able to recognize it. That is far more important. It has far more value. That is why we continue to go within ourselves, to break through that barrier between consciousness and subconsciousness and to awaken the psychic faculty.

A clairvoyant is considered to be able to see your past, your present, and the future. A psychologist can also do that, by allowing you to speak. He will understand the type of personality you are and can take a fairly clever guess as to your background and maybe even single out a specific event that has resulted in your present state. A clairvoyant can tap into something that has happened in your past and accurately assess your present state. When it comes to your future, however, that is where we have to be extremely careful, because the future is yet to happen and cannot be predicted.

With a fair understanding of the person's psychological makeup, one can "see" an event that is likely to affect the individual. Here, I am not attempting to contradict my earlier statement, where I said that one can foresee major events that are affecting locations, as opposed to individuals. In other words, in dealing with people, one has to deal with emotions, whereas events and locations can be treated objectively.

A psychic can foresee an event that may take place, as far as the individual is concerned, and can predict the outcome only as a result of an understanding of that person's psychological makeup, that is, how they would react, and so forth. Again, we are talking within the confines of our third-dimensional logic—the past, the present, and the inevitable (which we see as the future).

The future is inevitable. Specific events are not. Imagine a point, a dot. Call it the past. Imagine a second point two inches from the first. That is the present. Now make a third point to represent the future. Draw a line through all three dots. You have connected them, but you can still specifically pinpoint the past, the present, the future, separately, as designated by the three dots. Viewed from this dimension, one sees the straight line running through the three points. And one can logically see them as the past, the present, and the future. Looking down on the same line from yet another dimension—and rising higher—the line becomes shorter. So, the higher one rises, the shorter the line becomes until it is as one dot, that is, the past, the present, and the future, with no interval between them. This is what I believe the psychic achieves subconsciously. The psychic faculty enables him or her to rise to a nondimensional state, so that they are able to perceive all events, in one. To the untrained, this is akin to reading a book where all the words are there to be seen, but they are so jumbled and intermingled that it is impossible to make sense of the book. The trained psychic, however, is able to discern the various points.

To date, I have yet to be given a satisfactory explanation from any scientific authority as to how I (and other psychics who have attempted the same experiment) was able to predict in advance the identity of a person who would sit in a certain chair and to give accurate details about that person.

In giving the example of the line merging into one single point, according to the height from which one looks down on it, I am attempting to illustrate how the psychic is able to lower his or her vision—so that the three points become separate, once again, and because the range is not so great, that is, the line is shorter, the events (unlike the book of jumbled words) are quite clearly defined.

Time is of our own making. We are controlled by it and it is the most essential part of our day-to-day life. The primitive native is not so aware of the effect that time has on him but is aware of time as a natural, everyday event. The Earth goes around the Sun, bringing with it light and dark. And that is the only concept of time that the primitive knows and uses. In other words, time to get up, time to search for food, and time to sleep. We, conversely, are conscious of and are ruled by time. So that is something we must try to overcome when we are within our meditative state, or operating from a psychic viewpoint.

Even though we become psychically aware and are able to call ourselves psychic and to operate on that level, it still does not give us the complete answers. Many people ask me whether I can foresee death. Sadly, yes. I have seen death affecting people close to me, many times. It seems that I am contradicting myself here, where I have previously said that you can't see, or foretell, the future. I don't have any answer for that. I do not understand it, but I have felt the advent of an imminent death and it has, sadly, become a reality.

In many instances, there would seem to be a valid reason for my picking this up. I will quote the example of one of my closest friends, Tony. He was a young man, only forty-two, who had everything to live for. The only health problem he suffered from was diabetes. He tended to dismiss it as a debilitating illness and did not strictly keep to his prescribed diet. His friends always knew that if they were meeting Tony in a pub, he would first have injected himself with an extra boost of insulin, so he could take more alcohol into his system.

One day, I received a message that he had been taken into hospital. I went to visit him and he told me he felt he had abused himself with the insulin and should have learned his lesson. I left him quite chirpy and in good spirits. When I visited him the next day, to my horror I found that he was completely irrational. He barely recognized me. He was rambling and suffering from some form of delusion.

While I was there trying to rationalize and understand this, his wife Renee came in, and as we sat together, we watched him slip into some form of coma. We immediately called the nurse and Tony was rushed away.

At his wife's insistence, the doctor was summoned, and after being questioned, he told us: "He has cancer." We were shocked. We couldn't understand how it could happen without warning like this.

The doctor said that the cancer was terminal and that Tony had only six months to live. They would begin treatment on him the next day but would eventually send him home to die. It was believed he had

suffered some form of stroke. This was, they felt, a result of a reaction to the insulin.

When pressed for a more accurate prognosis, the
doctor said Tony would live between six and twelve
months. We were both devastated. As we walked away
from the hospital toward the car, we tried to absorb this
shocking news. I drove Renee back to her home. We
were lost in our private thoughts.

Then, Renee looked at me and said: "He can't suffer."

Without warning, I had a strange feeling we were
not alone. I visualized a nun. It was as if she were in the
car with us. I braked hard and stopped the engine. I
said: "Renee, he will die tonight!" I knew my friends
and knew I could talk this way. I couldn't have said this
to a stranger.

"Oh, thank God," she exclaimed. "I hope you are
right."

That night she rang me and said: "You were right,
Bob. Tony has died." It was a matter of forty-eight
hours between our visit to see Tony and the diagnosis
of cancer. And the postmortem revealed that the cancer
had spread and hit every part of his body. It was very
rapid.

Now, at the time I was well-known on the "Spiritualist circuit." At all times, I criticized those mediums
who claimed they had a guide—like a red Indian, a
nun, a doctor, simply because it absolved them of personal responsibility. Yet, it happened to me. I had a
strong vision of a nun, who mentally transmitted to me:
"We will take Tony tonight."

How do I explain this? The feeling of impending
death was very real and my own psychological reaction
to my best friend's illness, and imminent death, was
obviously affecting me. I was able to recognize what
doesn't exist—no-thing. That strong image of the nun,

which represented peace and serenity, came through to me. And that image enabled me to break away from my own emotion and to see clearly. Not to predict his death—but, to say quite simply, what was going to happen.

Chapter 4 The Search for Awareness

Let us try to understand what we mean by the term "awareness." It is an odd word, in that it can mean so much to different people. At its simplest level, we are aware of being because we can see and recognize. We are aware of each other. We are aware of our immediate third-dimensional environment.

Many years ago, I was introduced to a group that followed the teachings of one Meher Baba. This was in the early 1960s. Meher Baba was Indian by birth and had his home there, although he had, in the past two or three years, traveled quite extensively.

Initially, my reaction to this group was not a favorable one. They accepted Meher Baba as "the master." When one of the group spoke of him to me, he was referred to as "the master."

I couldn't go along with this. I could not accept this constant reference to "the master" when they greeted each other, or their almost dog-like devotion to him. But the one thing that impressed and attracted me was the fact that, for many years, he had not spoken to any one person. In fact, he did not communicate with people other than by a nod of his head or a smile.

When I was first brought into this cult, I was bombarded with literature. "the master" had issued this for us to read, the "master" had given us his latest gems of wisdom. I asked: "How can he do this, if he doesn't talk?"

The answer was: "He doesn't need to talk. He is able to communicate with those who are close to him, those who he has brought to a point of enlightenment. They, in turn, communicate, and are able to pass on his wisdom."

I am pleased now that his statement didn't cause me to give up immediately on Meher Baba. Something about him had reached out to me, but I felt that I could not become a cult member, having long ago accepted that any form of secular belief or religion is the biggest obstacle to achieving understanding or awareness.

All religions create division. And there is no such thing as a "true religion." Once again, I realize I could be skating on thin ice here and would seem to be denying what many people consider to be true. Theirs *is* the true religion. Theirs is the true way and if that is what they believe, they have a perfect right to do so. It would be extremely arrogant for me to try and impose my concepts upon them.

My aim, though, is to break away from any form of religion or secular belief. There is no necessity for it. I would quote what was purported to have been said (according to the Bible) by the man Jesus. Before his crucifixion, his disciples asked him: "Master, where are you going?" To which he replied: "In my father's house are many mansions. I go now to prepare a place for you."

Was he simply saying in my father's house there are many rooms, and if you believe and follow me, then I'll go and get the room ready for you when you die? Did he mean this? Or did those responsible for collating this magnificent book, the Bible, have a great awareness? Is it possible that the message that they wanted to convey

was that there are many religions and many beliefs—and that there is room for all of them? This is
what prompted me to go along with Meher Baba.

He did not claim to be "the master," but on being
questioned by one of his disciples, he communicated
that he accepted the term "avatar"—the awakener. All
the books that were purported to have come from him;
the thousands of words that were written as "Meher
Baba's teachings," were not his.

When he entered into silence, he had indicated
what he believed to be; that for him to achieve true understanding, for him to be able to have meaning, the
only way was for him to remain silent. Before he entered into silence, when questioned once again on his
awareness, he pointed all around him to indicate that
not only are we aware but *all* is aware—the trees, the
grass, the animals. All life, all "aware."

He claimed: "I do not have the greater awareness. On
the contrary," he indicated a boulder and said: "That
has greater awareness than you or I." The puzzled disciples asked how this was possible. Meher Baba replied: "Because it *is*, it has awareness, and the fact that
its awareness is greater than yours or mine is because it
is unaware."

One can well imagine the puzzled looks and the individual intellects, wanting to go a little further and
question this. But really, there is no need to. By his example of maintaining complete and absolute silence
and of communicating only by a gesture, was he hoping that, ultimately, even this would be superfluous?
That he would become the boulder? Complete in itself—in "being."

The words and books that were written and purported to be those of Baba were the works of those who
had been with him for many years; those who had sat at
his feet (before he entered his silence) and observed his

daily life, felt his serenity. It was they who presented the books and created the mystical father figure Meher Baba, denying what Baba wanted.

He was the awakener. By his example, I believe strongly that this was what he wanted.

For me, at the time, Meher Baba was extremely important. I do not advocate (unless you choose to do so of your own volition) that you should read or study his works, his life, or that of any other teacher or avatar, to the extent that I did. The most important and valuable thing I gained from Meher Baba—in respect of my own search—was a particular act that he was often witnessed to perform.

He had a great fondness for any person who did not appear to have normal intelligence and was unable to communicate in a conventional sense. One that we would call mentally deficient. He would wash them, feed them, cuddle them, love them, and, when he was questioned about this, he simply replied: "Do you know these people? What true awareness do they have? They are not the same as us, but are they not purer than us? Do they not have a simple trust? They do not have intellect. They cannot reason as we do, but does that make them inferior? Are they not closer to God in their awareness than you and I?"

Think about this.

At this point, I would recommend that you begin to place more emphasis on a deeper meditation.

Robbie Burns once said: "I would some gift the power give us to see ourselves as others see us." He was a very astute man, and I think we should take this as our next step toward discovering our psychic ability.

We are aware of who we are, at a physical level. Basically, we are also aware of our weaknesses, even though we put up psychological barriers to hide them from others. Many of us carry within us guilt and shame. We regret many things we have done in the past. In many instances, it is only you, the individual, who is aware of what you have done and what is considered to be wrong. But, is it wrong?

Try a little experiment. Each day, you look into the mirror, whether you shave or you put on makeup. Next time, before you do either of these things, simply look into the mirror and see yourself—look at yourself and be honest as to what you see.

You are seeing yourself but are you really looking beneath that psychological barrier, to see the complex character that you are? Take just one instance of where you feel guilt. Whatever that instance may be. What is it you feel guilty about? Is the guilt justified? Can you convince yourself that there was a reason for the action that has created this guilt? Can you perhaps blame it on another person, or on circumstances at the time?

It really doesn't matter. What you have done is in the past. There is no condemnation of any act that you may have committed. Society may well condemn you. Convention may condemn you. But, what is really important? The act that you have committed, whatever it was, should no longer concern you. It has gone.

You failed to conform to the dictate of norm that was decided for you. Is there such a thing as an act that can be called evil? Does evil exist as a separate entity? It cannot. Evil can only be the lowest manifestation of good. We are, once again, back to the concept of duality. You have committed an act that runs contrary to the norm of the society in which you have been placed. The guilt you now feel is important if you can accept it as a constant reminder of something you have experienced. The mere fact you feel guilt is an indication also of your remorse. You regret it; you wish you hadn't done it. As you develop, both intellectually and in maturity, you realize that what you did was wrong.

Some of the most horrendous crimes have been perpetrated by people, upon people. Society has created a structure where they can punish these crimes. I do not want to enter into a moral issue here. It is not your concern. Your concern is to concentrate only on yourself—to break through this morass of cross-wires that have been created by emotion and the concept of right and wrong.

You have experienced, and in that experience you have the opportunity to learn. Go back to the one experience that is causing you concern. It could be a family issue, or possibly, greater than that. Would you commit the same act again or have you learned from it? Have you not learned the lesson society would want you to learn? The lesson is: don't do it again. Conform. More important, have you learned within yourself? Do you recognize your mistake? Now is your opportunity to do so, for that is all that it was—a mistake. You have grown, as a result of that experience.

How many of you can look back and say "if only I'd done that, things would be different?" How many of you, when faced with a decision, are unable to make that decision? One person will advise you that this way is correct. Another will say: "No, this is correct." How do you know which is the correct decision to make? You don't. When the time comes for you to make a decision, you make it. Having made it, that decision is automatically right. It cannot be wrong. The die has been cast and the future has been determined by that decision. You cannot question yourself: "Did I make the right decision?" or say: "If only I had done that." That is in the past.

The question, again, of committing an act that runs contrary to the norm of society is a very difficult one for the individual to try and come to terms with, but nonetheless, it is for the individual to try to overcome that act.

You are now at a point in your life where your current circumstances and state of mind are a result of what has happened in the past. Is it possible you can repeat the same mistakes? Of course it is possible—if you accept that you made a mistake in the first place.

Rest assured that other people who have no awareness will condemn you more than you could condemn yourself. You must stand aside from that. There is no divine retribution. There is no "fiery furnace of hell," only the hell that you create within yourself, the hell that is created by your emotion. This is one of the most difficult stumbling blocks to overcome on your pathway toward awareness. But it is not insurmountable. It can be overcome, as your awareness increases, regardless of whether you deliberately set out to achieve awareness. But awareness grows with experience and you determine what is right or wrong. Invariably, what you determine to be right or wrong will conform to the dictates of society. It is not difficult to understand this.

It is your own awareness, through experience, that determines your actions. And to have achieved that awareness thus far, you must have erred. You obviously have made mistakes but you have committed no wrong, providing you recognize a mistake has been made. You are your own judge and jury and this is most important. Let others judge you as they will. Let others condemn you. If you can condemn yourself equally, then yours is the greater condemnation.

It is extremely difficult to try to put this across. I have said that I have no qualifications as a teacher. I do, however, have sixty years of life experience, the last thirty-five having been spent using a psychic faculty that I developed. I would argue that this is my qualification.

We all begin at the same level. As a child, you are like an empty vessel. The knowledge that is put into the vessel is what those with greater experience (so they would consider) have put in. Take the example of a child, perfectly happy in its environment, who, for the first time, is placed on the floor to learn to crawl. Crawling is a completely new experience for the child. The child has left its crib and the comfort and security of a mother's breast. It has now been placed in what must be akin to a completely new universe—the floor. The child can now see the colors of the carpet at close range. And as it begins to crawl and pull itself forward, the child comes across a tiny piece of dirt. It is an amazing discovery. Even greater is the discovery that the child can reach out and touch the dirt.

We all know that children invariably place everything they can pick up into their mouths—it is a basic primitive instinct. We know that it is dirty and unhygienic and we would automatically say to the child: "Don't."

Immediately we confuse the child. It may think: "Don't what? What have I done? I am experimenting. I am experiencing." We prevent that experience by saying "don't!"—because it is contrary to what we consider to be the norm.

From that first instance of the child being prevented from doing something, the child's natural awareness receives its first layer of the physical environment—what I would term grossness. As the child progresses through the various stages of its childhood, when it is taught to conform to the dictates of the environment in which it is placed, more layers are added.

True, life can still be an adventure, but even from the first time the child is told not to do something, it is like a seed that has been implanted. And, though the child may well attempt to repeat the act, it will make sure that no one is looking.

You can argue that this is necessary. It is right because we have to conform. There have to be rules and standards and we have to teach the child, of course. But is that all we are here for? Did not the child have a greater awareness? Think of Meher Baba's comparison to the stone.

Can we now condemn those who commit an act contrary to the laws of society? *Can* we? Is the psychologist correct in saying that there is a reason for the committing of that act, no matter how vile it may be? Emotionally, we may react against it. But, what is the reason behind the act? Is the person normal? Then again, are *we* normal? What *is* "normal"?

I can only hope as you read this that you have a very definite reaction to it and that you allow this reaction to come to the fore. To disagree with me violently is a good reaction. However, analyze why you disagree with me in such a forceful way.

I have asked you to look at yourself, to try to open up completely, so that you can look objectively at yourself and at your past actions—at your reactions to what I am saying. I am not asking you to bare your soul for all to see, only to yourself. In my first book, *Clues to the Unknown*, I wrote about myself. It was my autobiography. I told of the unhappiness I had created as a result of my first divorce. I still see, even now (when my children are well advanced into maturity), the reactions that my children have, the feelings and emotions that they contain within themselves because they did not have the solid security of a balanced relationship between their mother and father.

All these things I openly wrote about, because they were true. But did I bare myself completely? No. Am I to continue feeling guilty throughout my life, because I divorced my wife and caused my children anxiety? No. Why should I? Why should you, if you have had a similar experience. It is a decision that had to be made—and you made it. That decision was right. The result of that decision, though it may have an adverse affect on others, is not your guilt. It is not your responsibility. We each have to grow, as a result of what we experience. Too many people are not psychologically adjusted sufficiently to be able to achieve this. Perhaps that is the reason for the lack of moral attitude in today's society. I do not know. Am I to take responsibility? Are you to take responsibility? Can we defend our actions by saying we suffered a similar setback, as children? No. It is our own actions that we must stand by and if we can begin to come to terms with this, we will have a greater opportunity to remove these layers of grossness that prevent us from seeing the "real self," and within that real self, to see and recognize the driving force that is within us.

The ego is the most essential driving force of all. Contrary to popular opinion, you should never attempt to subjugate ego. It is essential. It is the "I am." It is the most important key toward success in achieving the psychic awareness.

We are all individuals and, though we pay lip service to it, I wonder how many of you really can embrace that simple fact of your own individuality? How many of you, at this point of your life, accept your role? Forget your everyday working life, which is essential to earn money for basic necessities. How many of you are parents, and from the day you became parents, how many accepted the role? When do you cease to become a parent? This is a very emotive subject. But, I ask once more, when do you cease to become "a parent"? Think about this. Where are you? The "I"— the "I am"— the individual. How can you manifest, if this mantle of responsibility that you assumed as a parent is to remain with you? It is a secondary role and soon that role must cease. The child will become self-sufficient. It will no longer need you. On the contrary, if you cannot recognize yourself as the most important, then you must accept that it is you that needs the child permanently. Rather, at all times, let the dominant feature be your own ego, that driving force toward achieving what matters to you.

Remember, the only positive statement that you can make is "I am." We can consider it our mantra, a mantra we repeat to ourselves constantly. Let it be that—"I am."

By now you should be ready for a slight variation in your meditation. As you enter into silence and concentrate on your breathing, mentally repeat to yourself, over and over again, "I am." If you have reacted against that which I have written, then it will become a good exercise for you to overcome it. Remember, my words are only the catalyst. If there is confusion and disagreement, it doesn't matter. Continue with the lesson.

Enter, then, into a few moments of quiet meditation by using the tape you have made and feel, slowly, the subtle changes that will take place.

Having practiced the opening and closing of the chakras and a short meditation by listening to the tape, you should now be able to approach the matter in a totally different perspective. You may still disagree, but you have had the opportunity to withdraw and now you can look at it a little more objectively.

Go back to your mirror. Look at yourself. Don't be afraid to look at yourself openly. It is only you who is going to see this. Be honest. Is this what you want to be? Do you want to achieve psychic awareness? Then look. There is nothing to be afraid of. It is you—but look deeper and "feel" the real you.

I hope that you have been playing tape one on a regular basis and that you have now become reasonably adept at being able to relax and enter within yourself, at opening and closing the chakras, and beginning to feel the subtle changes that take place.

So, let's try our first experiment, where you can prove to yourself the ability that is within you and you have an opportunity now to put it to a practical use.

Select two young plants, of your own choice, preferably ones that are suitable for indoor growth. Try to select two that are equal in size. They may be just beginning to put out shoots. When they have got a strong grip and are healthy, place them in separate pots and select one for your special concentration.

All that you need to do is water both plants equally, when necessary. Water one with ordinary tap water. But, as for the other plant, try this experiment. Fill a glass with ordinary water. Then hold your hand above the glass of water, about two inches away, and using the method you have now practiced, relax. As you begin to feel more at ease, concentrate on your hand that is hovering above the glass of water.

While you are concentrating on your hand, think of pushing energy toward the center of your hand. Concentrate on this. You should be able to feel a heat emanating from your hand. If you do not achieve this at first, do not concern yourself. Practice, until the whole of your concentration is on the hand that is held above the glass. Slowly you will feel the heat emanating from your palm. Concentrate on pushing this energy from your palm—without moving its position—into the water. Feel the energy flowing down your arm. Feel the energy generate heat, and project it into the water.

In time, you will feel this energy surging from you. After a minute, remove your hand and relax, simply by using your own breathing technique. Then pour the water into the plant that you have chosen as the recipient for the charged water (water the other plant with the same amount but use normal tap water).

55

You can also extend this experiment by tasting the water that you have charged and the water that has come straight from the tap. See if you can taste the difference. With practice and concentration, it should become quite easy. If you don't succeed in the first instance, by continual practice you will notice the difference between the water you have charged and the normal tap water. There is no question of doubt about it.

Observe the difference in the growth of the two plants. This will obviously take time but I am confident you will be quite amazed by the results. It is also an indication to you of the energy that can be projected from yourself, having broken through the first layer of the conscious mind.

Remember the example we gave earlier on, of the psychic who walks into a room where a murder has been committed, or the simple example of you, walking into a room where there has been an argument or some form of violent displacement of energy. You are now concentrating this energy into a practical purpose—that is all.

Many of you will experience a very definite sensation from your hand. A tingling of the fingers maybe. Do not be concerned. Concentrate on the experiment and gain confidence from it. It will obviously take time for you to see the effect on the two plants. The important thing is to treat them as normal. In other words, they may not need watering every day, but according to their requirements. Repeat the experiment, watering one with charged water and the other with plain tap water.

chapter 5 Defining the Paranormal World

Let us now discuss the terms that are commonly used within the psychic field. The most common is clairvoyance, which simply means clear vision. This does not necessarily mean that you are seeing events pictorially (though many clairvoyants, particularly mediums, claim that they do). I think for the purpose of our development, it is better to visualize mentally and, to understand this, it is important that you regularly practice mental perception. So, close your eyes whenever you have the opportunity and a few moments to spare and concentrate on an event or object—for example, a boat, gently bobbing on the sea.

Concentrate on this mental image of the boat—then free it from its anchor and sail away with it. The object of this exercise is simply to become accustomed to a mental concept, as opposed to a visual concept, for it is in this way that you will subsequently receive psychic impressions in your mind, as mental images, even as ideas or words. But do not expect to see these impressions as though you were looking at a television screen or viewing events as you normally would do through your eyes.

Another term used in the psychic field is clairaudi-ence, which simply means clear hearing. There are many exponents of clairaudience. The majority of these people operate and remain within the Spiritualist field, whereby they purport to hear voices that tell them of events or describe people. Again, it is not our intention to concentrate on this faculty. Our object is simply to concentrate on realizing the psychic faculty, or, as it is known, ESP (extrasensory perception). It may come in many forms.

On occasions, you may hear, or quite distinctly see, but in the main during our training program, ESP will come via the medium of mental perception. One im-portant aspect, however, that we will concentrate on is what is termed psychometry.

Psychometry is the ability to hold or touch objects that belong to people (personal affects, or artifacts, even pieces of wood or stone that have some historical connection) and, from the vibrations that emanate from such an object, pick up and interpret events and places.

If the object is a personal belonging, it is also possi-ble to diagnose physical and mental conditions, that is, the psychological state of the individual to whom the object belongs. This is one of the most important as-pects, because each and every one of you can practice this as you become more "aware" and more confident.

Psychics also use the term vibrations, meaning the power and energy that emanates from all things. For example, energy will remain in a room, buzzing and crackling, where a murder or some other violent crime has been committed. The same form of energy vibra-tions emanate from people.

A person can hand you a ring that they have been wearing. As you hold it, that ring becomes the person, with all the energy that they contain. By holding it, the psychic begins to receive mental images and can even take on physical conditions, such as a violent headache, some difficulty with blurred vision, a pain in the back, and so forth.

Very few people would realize that it is not a condition they themselves are experiencing, but it is the vibration emanating from the object they are holding. I think this is one of the fairest tests for any person who would claim to be psychic.

Scientists have used psychometry and psychics in an attempt to determine the history of objects that have been found in the ground. One particular psychic was given a piece of material that appeared to be fossilized stone. The psychic became confused—stating that he felt it to be from the Stone Age. Oddly enough, his dating was amazingly accurate. On being questioned further, he added: "It could be part of the bone of a dinosaur." Only the scientists knew it to be a fossilized bone of a Stone Age creature, as a result of DNA testing.

When the psychic was questioned as to why he had pinpointed the Stone Age, he said he had simply "seen" a mental picture of a caveman, but the longer he held it, the stronger became the vibration and the conviction that the object was part of a dinosaur.

There is nothing whatsoever to prevent you, the reader, as you begin to feel more confident, and as you play your psychic development tape on a regular basis, to practice this. Some of you may have instant success. Others may experience greater difficulty because you have yet to overcome the psychological barrier.

This can be a very difficult hurdle to overcome, but, with practice, you will achieve it. You will receive your own interpretations and will achieve eventual success. With this success will come a greater sense of self-confidence.

Once you have listened to your tape and achieved a relaxed state of mind, practice psychometry. Take hold of an object belonging to somebody who can confirm your "reading." Hold the object and allow the sensations and vibrations to flow into you. If any mental image is formed, reveal it. If you experience any form of pain or discomfort, fear, stress, joy—reveal it. Obviously, it would be better if you could perform this psychic development exercise with a stranger, because if the object belongs to a partner or friend, one could argue that you are picking up what you already know. The ultimate test would be in holding an unknown object, with no preconceived ideas in your mind.

Try taking a stone. Hold it in your hand and see what you can take from it, what you feel from it. The important thing is to practice. To become confident in your own ability. Try it with any object that has its own identity. Experience the vibrations.

It is also important (even though you may feel that after listening to the cassette a few times, you really haven't achieved anything) to analyze, each and every day, starting with your home environment.

By now, you will have begun to develop. You began to develop when you first accepted the premise that the psychic faculty is within each and every one of you. You began when you first used the tape to take yourself into these layers of consciousness beyond the conscious mind.

Every day, after waking, most people go through a normal routine, of washing, having breakfast and getting ready to face the day. They allow no time for anything else. But, try to spend a little time with yourself every morning. Analyze how you feel each day. This is most important. If you are feeling unwell, you now know a simple remedy, which the tapes have indicated. You can now relax for a few minutes. Become aware of the importance of your ego. Become aware of the necessity to have a positive attitude.

Then, analyze the atmosphere of your home. Without your partner having said anything, you may well sense something is not quite right. Maybe he or she is not feeling too well. Maybe there is something troubling your partner. Maybe he or she will speak of this and you will find it confirms your own impressions.

We have already discussed people who are close to each other being aware (on what we would term a "hunch level") of something not being quite right. We now know that this hunch level is our own psychic faculty operating, so it is important to practice using it.

On the occasions when you use public transport and find yourself sitting next to somebody, instead of being totally immersed in your journey or locked in your own thoughts, spend a little time relaxing and concentrating on any one person who is traveling in the same train compartment or on the same bus. See what you can pick up. It is obvious you cannot go and ask them for confirmation, but it is still a worthwhile exercise for your own development and awareness.

Select any one individual. By looking at them and concentrating, begin to sense and feel what type of personality they are. You should begin to form a psychic impression, perhaps concerning the way they are feeling, or the way they live their life.

This is a valuable exercise to perform every day, even within your work environment. Try to analyze the different moods that your work colleagues are projecting, to sense their feelings. What has happened to them to cause their present condition or state? You will now begin to understand much more. You will begin to understand other people as a result of finding self-awareness.

When you arrive home from work, you enter into a

familiar environment. Unless something dramatic has occurred, you will usually be unaware of any subtle changes that may have taken place within that atmosphere. Maybe your partner has become a little screwed up, because of a frustrating day? Nothing too serious maybe but, nonetheless, it alters the peaceful vibrations.

Analyze any environment into which you enter. See if you can determine the vibrations within. We know that clear vision (or clairvoyance) is not seeing with the eyes. So, try to accept the analogy of a bowl of water.

You can see right through to the bottom of the bowl. The water is transparent and undisturbed. But, if you should drop a stone into the water, it will have a rippling effect and the whole surface will change. You create a wave effect. The bottom of the bowl is still visible, but the vision is disturbed.

Go back to the tape, where you were sitting in a semimeditative, relaxed state. Remember what took place, the sharp noise that disturbed you, how your whole aura became a jangled mess. Compare that with the bowl of disturbed water.

Most environments (including our home or dwelling environments) carry the vibrations of those people within them. It only takes a small incident, a slight mishap, to cause those vibrations to jangle, the same as dropping the stone into the bowl of water. The water within the bowl will take some time to settle, but the surface will eventually become still, as before. Likewise, the disturbed vibrations within a room will return to normality.

I would suggest that your home is perhaps the easiest and most readily available environment for you to practice your perceptions. It is early days yet to anticipate anything dramatic taking place but, at this point, one word of warning. Your first steps taken, when you listened to the tape and practiced your breathing (when you concentrated on the chakras), you created, without any question of doubt, a hole through the barrier of your conscious and subconscious mind.

At the end of each session of meditation, you have been taught how to close down the chakras and to close the aura. It is most important that you do this. It is very unlikely that, at this early stage, you will be called on to experience a highly disturbed environment that could cause a violent shock to your solar plexus chakra. But it can happen. There is nothing to fear. It can happen to those who have taken no positive steps in training, as you have done so far, but the most important thing to remember is to relax. Concentrate on your breathing and let that become your focal point. Bring it up from the solar plexus and close down the chakras very positively. You will then be able to return to normal day-to-day reality. Do not be concerned. There is nothing adverse that can happen to you. The shock you would experience is no different from that of receiving bad news. It can devastate anybody. But if it should be of a psychic nature (as a result of your testing out environments and atmospheres), then withdraw from it. Relax and close down. Analyze each event and each occurrence. As you analyze, you will become used to separating it from any physical reaction and recognize it as psychic perception.

I would offer another word of warning. Do not become sidetracked into other aspects of the paranormal. There is nothing wrong with this fascinating field and the wide range of subjects it encompasses, but each and every aspect has a different slant to it and can be somewhat confusing.

For example, if you are studying Greek and decide to study German and French at the same time, you will have tremendous difficulty in being able to concentrate on one particular language. In trying to learn three different languages all at once, you will probably find yourself mingling the three together.

So, try not to get too involved or sidetracked. There are so many diverse opinions on this subject that it is easy to become confused. I am not trying to tell you that this is the only path to self-awareness. However, I am simply passing on thirty-five years of personal experience, revealing to you what has worked for me and thousands of other people. Once you feel you have achieved some success from this book, then, and only then, would I advocate the study of other aspects and allied subjects.

There are hundreds of subjects that come under this broad umbrella known as the paranormal, each fascinating in its own right, and too many people make the mistake of trying to embrace the whole thing.

Extrasensory perception (the psychic faculty) comes under this umbrella, and if you can accept with an open mind that all things are possible, without becoming sidetracked, then that is the best viewpoint.

Later, as you begin to feel and achieve your own awakening of the psychic faculty, your own awareness will determine which direction is the right one for you. It will, I am sure, be impossible for you to ignore all aspects of this vast subject. It is fascinating, absorbing and mind-boggling. But, as the old saying goes, let us crawl before we can walk.

I would rather concentrate on first achieving awareness and, having achieved it, look at the beneficial aspects of it. As you practice your experiment with the plants, just think of the possibilities that lie within that one simple act of placing your hand open and discharging energy from it.

Think of the phenomena that is known as spiritual healing. I, personally, would prefer to drop the word "spiritual" and would rather term it "psychic healing":

the application of psychic energy—psychic power. I will discuss psychic healing and its practitioners at greater length later in the book. For now, I am keen to tackle this thorny subject of attaching the "spiritual" to what I believe is a natural, inherent psychic ability within us all.

Some clairvoyants become dependent on the use of a crystal ball through which to focus their attention. They believe that, without this crystal ball, they are unable to operate. It is their focal point in which they purport to be able to "see" events, but they don't actually see anything within the ball. They are simply operating in the same psychic manner as we are. They do not need the psychological prop. It is the same with spiritual healing. "Spiritual" is defined as that which emanates from the spirit, that which emanates from the power of God. This I do not accept.

The power, the energy—what was and what we can find in the circle that we recognize, is the energy into which you are tapping. It is the energy that you are and it is for you to learn to control it, to focus it in a positive manner.

As with duality, there has to be a negative side as well, and this energy can be misused, that is, misused as in the expression of anger. As we have discussed earlier, it is all too easy to get into a violent rage, to shout and curse, thus releasing intense energy in an explosion. The energy is not being directed in a positive way and therefore can only have an adverse affect.

But think again of that violent energy, being transmitted in a positive flow. There is a story that I like and that I think might sum this up. It concerns a little raindrop that is falling in a shower of rain and finds itself isolated and caught up in the wind. The wind carries the solitary raindrop over the land until it eventually passes over the ocean. At that time, there was a violent storm blowing and the waves were reaching ten or fifteen meters high and crashing down with a frenzy, creating great energy and noise.

The little raindrop looked down on all this activity and thought: "This must be the mighty powerhouse. This must be God, the center of all energy."

The sea looked up and saw the raindrop and said: "Come, join me."

I think we should also touch on another aspect of this vast field, one that causes many people, particularly those of the orthodox religions, a great deal of anxiety. The belief that we, the adept psychics, are playing with fire. The fear that we are tapping an energy, a power, that we do not understand.

My answer to this accusation would be in the form of a question. Do they understand this power? There can be no doubt that, should a survey be taken, the majority of people questioned on this subject would be found to have some interest (bordering upon fascination) in the paranormal—the "unknown."

Some of the most popular films and books are based on the writer's concept and imagination about the paranormal and the unknown. Why is this? Why are the sceptics so ready to reject it? Scientists throughout the world have now begun to take an active interest in the subject and many universities have set up facilities wherein they can investigate this phenomena, particularly that of the psychic.

In the past, their approach to this subject has been somewhat limited in as much as they continued to ask for repeatability. They would witness a psychic producing some paranormal effect and, having experienced the demonstration, they would dismiss it as possibly random, demanding repeat performances.

You have probably seen or read about psi cards, which contain five symbols. Time and time again, the scientists place emphasis upon these as having some importance. They will shuffle a pack of cards containing these five symbols and turn them over one by one, asking the psychic to predict what symbol the next card will reveal.

These tests have been repeated over and over again. What an absolute waste of time. In the main, the evidence pointed to a strong degree of perception—that the results outweighed the possibility of random chance. But that seems to be as far as they are prepared to go. Over the past ten years, however, great progress has been made. Unfortunately, a great number of the investigations that have been carried out under scientific conditions have proven to be so dramatic that the findings have not been released to the public. In particular, when the American military became involved. It is a known fact that they have used psychics in competition with the Russians, who have set up vast training schools for anyone showing the slightest glimpse of psychic ability. Imagine where this could lead. Think of the value of ESP in the field of espionage.

Putting this thought to one side, however, it has been of extreme benefit to establish that the psychic faculty does exist within certain individuals. In Russia, anybody who shows the slightest ability (particularly in sports) is removed from his or her normal environment and placed in an extremely cloistered one, where the whole emphasis is on training that person to the peak of fitness and ability.

The whole object is to win, to be the best. So one can imagine—although there is no evidence available to support this—that this same approach was taken with those who showed some psychic ability. In fact, much of the recorded data, which is available on film, comes from Russia. Even today, scientists agree that the results shown on this film footage are 100 percent genuine.

Scientists have conducted studies of people who have the ability to control inanimate objects. They have placed a needle under a sealed glass dome and put psychics in test conditions—to use their concentration and move the needle. The extremely rigid scientific conditions do not allow any possibility of fraud or deception.

This has been of tremendous value and one can only hazard a guess as to what is currently happening within these cloistered environments of scientific study. However, I maintain that we all have this psychic ability within us, though not all of us have the inclination (or opportunity) to develop it to such a pitch, bearing in mind that most of us are immersed in a materialistic environment, whereas the subjects of such exacting experiments have been removed from their environments and have been placed in conditions where they have no outside distractions.

But, even in establishing the psychic faculty at its very basic level, think of the tremendous advantages it can provide, not only to you as an individual, but within your own environment, to your family, and to society. It can lead to a greater understanding of other people and, following it to its natural conclusion, it will ultimately reflect on those of the future and of future generations, who will be brought up with a natural acceptance of the psychic faculty. It need not be contained under the heading "paranormal," nor regarded as "fascinating but dangerous." It will become a natural development, part of our everyday life, and who knows what benefits we can ultimately achieve with this faculty?

I know what I have achieved. It has been recorded and well documented. What I do not know is how much I am able to achieve. What are my limits? What example can I give? What test can be devised?

I am prepared to accept any challenge. I am not guaranteeing that I will achieve results—but I am certainly open to attempt any experiment, so that we can expand the horizons of our knowledge. As stated, scientists have limited their research into the psychic to laboratory conditions and laboratory tests. Would it not be of greater value for the scientists to come out of their laboratories and become involved in a more practical way? Let us take, for example, the psychic detective involved in crime. Let the psychic and the scientist work together. When a psychic is asked to become involved in a criminal investigation or to solve a mystery where conventional methods have drawn a blank, let the scientists witness the psychic at work and form their own opinions—under test conditions—to see the results, at first hand, of the psychic faculty operating at a normal level (normal, that is, to the psychic).

The scientist could then analyze the results and collate all the evidence that has been given by relating it to evidence known only to the police, and thereby strictly assess its accuracy.

Surely this way would be of greater value. No scientist in a laboratory can locate the source of the psychic faculty. They can theorize but, by observing psychics, they are seeing at first hand a faculty that is being used at a natural level.

Between them, the scientist and the psychic could be equally responsible for eradicating this fear and rejection of the word "psychic."

We can all marvel and be impressed by modern-day stage magicians and, in many instances, the effects are so dramatic that they defy logical explanation. Yet, this stage magician will admit that his magic is an illusion.

Scientists view the psychic with the same cynicism and will continually look for some form of deception—

hence the security they feel in isolating the psychic in laboratory conditions. But they are achieving little. It would be far better for them to work together, over an agreed period, and the results could be collated and assessed. True, they will only be able to say: "Yes, this man has achieved success as a result of his psychic ability." They will not be able to pinpoint the location of that faculty within him and no doubt they will regard this psychic as something of an oddity, something abnormal. This is why I insist that I am not unique— and that the faculties I have found within myself are indeed there to be discovered within each and every one of us.

chapter 6 My Search for Awareness

My main emphasis throughout has been that I am not unique or gifted. So, how did I become aware of my own psychic faculty? My earliest memories, as a child, are from a time when I was about five years of age and, along with thousands of other children from London, was evacuated to Nottingham to escape the effects of the German bombing.

Unlike the many children who grew up within a family that offered love and security, I was one of the unfortunate ones, in that I was foisted upon a family of strangers—who took me grudgingly and regarded me as an unwelcome addition to the household.

As for myself, I cannot remember any feelings of regret, remorse, or confusion at being taken away from my mother. Reflecting back on those troubled times and my early life, I have come to understand why. I had never really lived with my mother.

I was an illegitimate child who was virtually fostered out by her from the age of six months. So I had no knowledge of what a child from a normal family environment experienced. One can argue that, psychologically, I had blocked out that part of my life. But, I would argue that, although I hadn't found it to be of great importance to me at the time, I obviously felt the need to know who my father was.

As a small child, along with many others, I succumbed to psychological pressures and disorders and on a regular basis would wet my bed, which made my foster parents tremendously angry. Even now, I can remember quite clearly (and I bet the psychologists will have a field day with this) being knocked from the top of the stairs to the bottom on a regular basis, and of being wrapped in the urine-soaked and dripping sheets while I drank a cup of tea and ate a slice of bread before I went to school. I was not allowed to wash myself and was therefore forced, time and time again, to sit in class smelling of urine. What a treat for the other children.

Later on, at the age of seven, I became the subject of sexual abuse by the eldest son of the family and was terrified of being left alone at night with this young man. I desperately sought to find an escape. But I was just a child; there was no obvious way out. I didn't have any close friends and certainly couldn't confide in the family. On reflection, I can now see quite clearly that, at the tender age of seven, my psychic faculty was already operating.

I knew, for example when I came home at night, whether I was going to be alone in the house with my abuser because my foster mother was out. On other occasions, I knew that it was safe to enter the house because she was there. I was already able to anticipate events that were going to take place.

As was common with the children of that time (particularly those who were not in conditions where they were able to be scrupulously clean), I eventually caught lice in my hair. I was taken to a clinic where my head was completely shaved and covered with a violet paint. I was quite a startling sight—totally bald with a violet blue head.

The common headgear during these war years was a flying helmet—a plastic helmet, balaclava-style, that covered the head. The clinic supplied me with one of these and I wore it to school the next day. The teacher called the roll, and when I answered to my name, she regarded me long and hard and ordered me to remove my unbecoming hat.

I refused. After repeating her request three times, she strode down the classroom toward me. I can still remember the look of intense anger on her face because I had dared to disobey her.

She ripped the helmet off my head. That moment imprinted itself on my mind and probably became the most important event of my life. I saw in this teacher's eyes her horror at what she had done to me, and the utter wretchedness that followed her anger.

She rushed out of the classroom, leaving behind her the laughter of the children as all eyes turned on me and my colorful head. But all this seemed unimportant, because something had happened to me in that moment. My concern was not for my own discomfort but for the misery of that teacher. I had witnessed a projection of love in a way that, as a child, I hadn't seen before. I couldn't understand the way it was affecting me.

Later that day, I was called to the headmaster's office and the matter was smoothed over, in some way or another. I really wasn't concerned, but the teacher did not appear for the rest of that day.

That evening, she came to my foster parents' home and asked to see me. She was told that I was outside somewhere. She chose not to wait in the house (I would imagine this was because she had seen for herself the circumstances in which I was living). She eventually found me in the street and invited me to go for tea at her home that Sunday afternoon.

Joy of joys. Somebody was taking an interest; somebody who was prepared to extend something that was new to me. Love. I was still completely in awe of this teacher and couldn't understand the feeling I had received from her, but I knew there was nothing to fear and that I could have complete trust in her.

So, I went to her home for Sunday tea. It is strange what remains in one's mind from childhood, but I vividly remember her asking me whether I would like to play with a toy train set. This, of course, was a child's dream during the war years. To my surprise and delight, she had a railway set laid out in the room next door. I remember being overjoyed and absolutely amazed at being allowed to play there for the next few hours.

Afterward, I was invited to sit down and eat bread, butter, and jam and even cakes. It was a wonderful and rare experience for me.

Later on, she asked me if I would like to go to chapel with her. Until then, apart from the basic religious instruction that all children have at school, I had not had any connection with the church. To me, priests were simply people who were separate from us, who had no control or effect on my life at that time.

But I trusted this woman, so I went to chapel with her and it was there, as a bewildered child, I first came into contact with Jesus, not as a spiritual being—but as a father/mother figure.

I did not see Jesus as the son of God, or of any great spiritual significance. To me, Jesus was simply a friend. He was someone who was there when I faced the terrors of the night, as all children do at some stage, but more so with me, because I was locked in a dark room and dreaded hearing the footsteps of my abuser coming up the staircase and unlocking my door.

From that night, I was no longer afraid of the dark. The dark became inviting. I was able to become as one with the night, I was able to talk to this Jesus figure. I was able to free myself and bring all my miseries to the surface. Yet, I maintain that I was not psychologically maladjusted.

From that point on, my playtimes took on a different meaning. I had been used to sitting in corners, longing to be invited to join the other children on the cricket or football teams. I knew that if there were a sufficient number of players, I was not going to be selected by either side. On the rare occasions I was selected (it was pure necessity that prompted them), I remained a constant source of ridicule.

But now my play became more significant. I was happy to be alone. I had my horse. I was Roy Rogers; I was whoever I wanted to be. I could disappear completely into my own little world. It was then that I began to experience vibrations around me, to analyze and absorb.

The celebrated author Colin Wilson emphasizes that this experience was the beginning of my isolation (as he would term it) from conventional society. I became what he termed an "outsider." It was this emotional upheaval that jolted my psychic awareness and brought it to the fore.

Until I met Colin Wilson, I had never considered this. At first I was simply honored that he should write an introduction to my book, *Clues to the Unknown*. It was only afterward that I realized he had put his finger on the whole thing; the fact that many psychics and many "sensitives" discover their abilities as a result of some emotional event that has taken place in their lives.

I am convinced that people who are confined to wheelchairs as a result of a disability or following an accident and have little else to do but to sit, due to their immobility, and have a strong awareness of the psychic field and of their psychic faculty. I am sure that they operate this faculty daily; that their loneliness is not increased by being alone with their thoughts but, rather, that their psychic ability is enhanced as a result of having been confined within a wheelchair—and within their own loneliness.

At the time of my first awareness, I had no concept or intelligent appraisal of being psychic in any way. To me, these things were natural and they continued to be natural until it reached a point where, at the age of twenty-one, I began to be at odds with other people and to put forward certain questions and theories as to why other people didn't feel like I did, why they didn't believe what I believed.

I was constantly told by my elders that all this questioning was only a sign of youth and immaturity and that I would grow out of it in time and change my views. I never did. I could not understand at the time. Now, on reflection, I can and it is from that point in my life that I began to develop. A very significant time for me.

I constantly reiterate that I know what I can do, but I don't know what I can't do. This is why I have maintained that it is for other people, particularly those with an analytical brain like Colin Wilson's, to be able to look and analyze clearly and concisely—and to be able to advance the possibilities.

Having begun to react to certain conditions and environments from an early age without knowing it, I began to question what was happening to me. Why did I feel so different? I had no concept of the psychic faculty. I had heard of people who could predict the future, but this wasn't what I was doing. I was simply sensitive to atmospheres and environments and I reacted instinctively against them—to such an extent that it ultimately took me to a point where I had what can only be termed a breakdown.

As a result, I came up against psychologists for the first time and I quickly realized that they had but one objective in mind. That was to bring me back to the state (and narrow confines) of "normality." They were not interested in looking at the possibility of me being psychic. My behavior was defined as being antisocial, but this gave me no comfort nor did it help me to understand. Therapy was of no value to me. I had to find someone who could explain what was happening to me.

Eventually, I was taken to a medium, who clarified everything in one brief meeting by simply telling me: "You are psychic. That is your 'problem.'" She was able to explain to me that it was certain traumatic events that had created my confusion. I grasped at this explanation like a drowning man does at a straw. I allowed myself to be drawn into a Spiritualist environment, which, without any question of doubt, was the first solid foundation to my future security. Fortunately, it also gave me the ability and opportunity to question—and, from the answers, to interpret.

As my own awareness developed, I began to seek other avenues in which the psychic faculty could be important. I became fascinated by mysteries, particularly involving crime, murder, and the disappearance of children. I was able to apply my "talents" in a way that they would be of practical value to society.

In writing this chapter, it has been my intention throughout to remove any impression that I am setting myself up in the role of a teacher or guru. I would certainly not want to be considered as having any involvement in helping people to achieve that which is termed "spiritual" awareness.

My message is simple and if you find it repeated throughout the book, it is because I feel it is the only one that I can emphasize. The psychic faculty is normal—latent in each and every person—and it can be developed very easily.

I believe that, on average, three in every ten people use their psychic awareness in some way or another. But these three-in-ten must begin to accept that they have this ability—and therefore that they can use it on a practical level in their everyday life, without cluttering their minds with "pseudospiritual" beliefs and involvement.

There are far too many spiritual philosophies that run parallel with each other but, in a sense, each has some truth. I suppose my message, quite simply, is to beware of false gurus. As previously stated, there seems today to be a general awakening, a general need for people to seek beyond their material existence and to find justification and meaning in their own lives.

In 1990 I withdrew from the psychic scene and came to Cyprus to live with my wife, Jen. For six years, I lived a life of complete anonymity. No one knew who I was or what I was and, for six years, I had the opportunity to analyze my past experiences, to be able to analyze myself more deeply, and to come to a far deeper understanding of myself than I ever had in the past.

I was able to write a book, for commercial gain, concerning my experiences as a psychic detective, investigating cases all over the world. But still this did not give me satisfaction. And I pondered on the writing of this current book for some time. Had it not been for some strange quirks of fate, maybe it would not have been written.

Having been able to remain anonymous in this small and usually peaceful island of Cyprus, blessed with sunshine for 330 days of the year, my existence has been almost idyllic. But it didn't seem enough, my achieving this self-satisfaction and being at peace, "at one" with the world. I was aware, as a result of the media, of all the trials and tribulations and the problems that beset our world today, some very close to "home," in fact, concerning Cyprus itself.

Cyprus is an island that was forcibly divided in 1974. A Turkish occupation force took over more than a third of the island and still remains in situ. Cyprus itself, and the Cyprus mentality, suited me. It has a very strong religious leadership and ties. It is Greek Orthodox, a major branch of the Christian world, and it is fair to say that the church plays an extremely important part in the day-to-day life of the average Cypriot.

It is certainly not for me to criticize the power of the church in Cyprus; neither have I felt the necessity to sit and discuss with Greek Orthodox Cypriots the rights or wrongs of religion in today's world. In fact, it is an extremely emotive subject to deal with. Bearing in mind that the invaders who occupy over a third of the island are Muslim, and there is no question of doubt that the gulf between the Muslim and the Christian world is so wide, it seems that centuries must pass before a mutual understanding can be achieved.

However, in the past two years I began to notice small advertisements starting to appear in a local English-language newspaper, the *Cyprus Weekly*. People were advertising services like tarot readings, psychic consultations, private sittings, and astrological readings. I thought this somewhat odd, although I realized there was quite a large British expatriate community on the island.

This surge of interest began to increase, to the point where the Greek Orthodox church felt the need to issue public announcements to their "flock," to have nothing to do with what can be loosely termed the "New Age" arts. But still the New Age practitioners advertised their services and many well-known mediums began to visit the island. The common theme of them all was helping people to achieve self-awareness.

As a matter of interest, I began to investigate the current situation in Britain and I was absolutely amazed by the tremendous resurgence of interest in these matters, not only in Britain but also the United States of America. It was as if the so-called "dawning" of the Age of Aquarius was imminent, as we approach the millennium.

The more I studied this phenomenon, the more concerned I became. It seemed as if people were desperately seeking an alternative to materialism, normality. I personally believe that religion has no place in today's society. Yet, what are we going to put in its place? I don't feel there is a need for any replacement.

This awareness is part of our natural growth, part of our human physical development. I am quite confident of this. As our intelligence increases, as the boundaries of medicine and science are pushed further and further back and we become aware, as a result of instant communication, we can see quite clearly that there are far too many things that are beyond our comprehension—yet that cannot be dismissed.

One of the most popular television programs of late, which has prompted many books and articles, is *The X-Files*. This is a work of fiction, based upon elements of truth, and it has caught the public's imagination all over the world. Almost anything with a mention of *The X-Files* seems to be guaranteed automatic commercial success. Why is this?

Is it because we know, within ourselves, that these things can, and do, exist? In which case we have to restructure the whole of the last 2,000 years of thought and belief. The Christian church no longer holds the power that it used to and we should be excited by the onset of this major change.

We have recently heard from eminent scientists that their investigations now indicate the possibility that a crude form of life once existed on Mars, a planet in our solar system that is further away from the Sun than the Earth is. Many people say that they already believe this, so why should this revelation be so earth-shattering? I believe this is earth-shattering because it undermines many of our previously held assumptions. We can no longer remain insular, or consider ourselves unique.

Seventy years ago, the thought of man being able to travel through space was strictly the domain of the science fiction writers. It became science fact thirty years later. We have now sent spacecraft to the very edge of our solar system. We are discovering other galaxies, analyzing new data. The whole subject is almost mind-shattering. The possibilities are endless. We are now looking for something to hold onto—something tangible. Some people find it difficult to come to terms with these possibilities and to embrace all these theories. These scientific breakthroughs, which have taken us beyond a point we ever dreamed possible, may even make us feel uncomfortable.

The fact remains that these changes are gathering pace—and I think that this has got to be the most exciting thing of all. It should help you, the reader, to come to terms, more and more, with what we have discussed and are beginning to practice and put into effect.

Make no mistake about it—the psychic faculty is going to become one of the most important issues in tomorrow's world. Yet, it is not a new discovery; it has always been there, waiting to be fully appreciated, as has the possibility of discovering life on other planets, or perhaps the likelihood of interstellar travel. Our new scientific knowledge gives us the ability to turn the science fiction of the six-million-dollar bionic man into science fact. All that was ever needed was the intelligence and the awareness to develop and broaden; to be able to embrace the possibility.

Now, the challenge for you, the reader, is to accept the fact that the psychic faculty is latent in each and every one of you, as you continue with your own personal development. As science looks outward, we must look inward.

chapter 7 The Psychic Wilderness

I once had occasion to be working in a hospital for the severely subnormal. I have written about this experience before but, nonetheless, I think it is important to examine it again because I believe it enhances my theory concerning what I term the "psychic wilderness."

There was a young man of twenty-one at the hospital. His name was Peter and he had stopped growing, both physically and mentally, at the age of three. His limbs were bent and twisted and he could neither move nor communicate in any way whatsoever. His daily routine consisted of being fed and having the excrement wiped from his body—over which he had absolutely no control.

Peter suffered from epilepsy. One day he was launched into a series of epileptic fits, one after another. His poor body was thrown all over the place and he was rapidly drained of energy. During the last attack, he died.

I was with him while he was going through this devastating experience. While he was in this state of epileptic seizure, he communicated with me. I cannot explain how; there was no word or written message. It was simply a communication that he was there and that what was taking place, these violent spasms, was not affecting him. Despite the physical shaking and thrashing we witnessed, the communication that I received from him was that he was separate from it.

This experience with Peter made me question and analyze other victims. What is really taking place in the mind of a person who is in a coma or semivegetative state? The medical profession is able to register brain activity and is able to determine that the person is alive. Brain activity can be confirmed and recorded by eye movement.

But nothing will convince me that these are involuntary spasms. I am convinced that, within this coma state, these people are alive—I find this possibility very exciting and feel it should be investigated thoroughly by the medical community. Coma victims continue to live but in a way that we do not now accept or properly understand.

I feel that, in this state, they are within that psychic field of energy that I am trying to explain in this book. There is no mystery. They are within the "psychic wilderness." The psychic wilderness cannot be measured in relation to physical distances. It is all around us, like a layer of atmosphere around a planet. All vibration, all thought, all deeds are there. Everything is there.

On the edge of the psychic wilderness is a level where I believe those in a coma go. This is where they exist. This is my theory and I hope that you will "look" for yourselves—and begin to devise from it your own level of awareness.

Has not science put forward the theory that there is also a parallel world to ours; a world that occupies the same amount of space, at exactly the same time—of equal mass—but vibrating at a totally different speed? This hypothesis has been investigated. Does science put any boundaries on its quest for knowledge, for awareness? No. Then why should you put any boundaries on yourself and your quest for psychic awareness?

What this book has done, and what it will continue to do, is to awaken you to the solid reality that the psychic faculty has no mystery. It is there; we are part of it—and we can use it constantly to beneficial effect, because now we begin to accept that it is our mind, it is us within that mind, that controls our body.

The word "phenomenon" would not normally be applied to sleep, but if you think about it, it is a phenomenon—albeit a natural one. Our body closes down as a result of the need for recharging its energies; we need to sleep.

Science has conducted, and continues to conduct, experiments into sleep and into the patterns of sleep. Scientists can clearly define the level of sleep into which we have slipped. The brain pattern can be recorded and rapid eye movement (which indicates dreams) can be monitored. We all dream.

One of the more modern ways of psychic reading is the interpretation of dreams. I think, however, that those who put themselves up as "dream analysts" are treading on very thin ice. There are, on certain levels, dreams that can have a definite relation to your present situation. But the deeper we go, the deeper we enter into a strange twilight world, where there is neither rhyme nor reason for what we are experiencing. Even the sexual dreams. We have all experienced these. Many times, there seems to be no reason for our choice of partner, or partners, within these dreams. There seems to be no connection with us, whatsoever. The person you dream about may be a complete stranger, with no bearing on anyone we know in our day-to-day lives.

Similarly, we experience dreams that take us to far horizons. They make sense within themselves, and yet when we become fully aware and are operating on a physical level, we find ourselves unable to interpret the dream. We don't know exactly why, but we do know that in that dream state we have complete freedom. We are unrestricted, uninhibited.

The reason I believe the modern psychic analysts of dreams are skating on thin ice is because of their assumption that sleeping and dreaming is relative to our physical state of existence, that is, the third-dimensional state. How can they assume that?

When we are consciously active, in our day-to-day life, there can be clearly defined levels of awareness and normality and of going beyond the norm, in some other action. When we sleep, however, we are unfettered, unrestricted by convention—even by our own moral code. We go beyond that.

There are certain arguments that, when we dream at a certain level, a psychological interpretation has value, particularly for those suffering from stress.

I cannot be certain about my theory. I will know, at some future time, but as to whether I will be able to communicate it is another question. Happily, medical science can alleviate the pain of most people with terminal illness. They can induce sleep with drugs. They can numb the body. But they cannot numb the mind.

In applying drugs to alleviate pain, where do they "send" the patient? What happens to the person after the drugs have been administered and they are asleep?

Sleep, throughout the ages, has always been considered as having the finest recuperative powers possible. But what provides this refreshment? Is it because the body is still and resting? Or, has the body separated from the mind?

Astral projection, or out-of-body (OOB) experience, is now widely accepted by scientists and the medical profession. It is based on the premise that we have an ethereal counterpart to our physical body and that, as we sleep, it leaves the physical body and hovers above it, where it is then charged.

Most scientists will attempt to debunk the theory of psychic energy. But they accept that the astral body leaves the physical for recharging—like a battery. Charged with what? What is this state—and where is the mind? Is the mind within this astral state?

The astral state is considered by many to be one of the lowest states of existence outside the physical. The theory is that the more gross a life a person has led, the lower the astral plane to which they will go.

We all enter into this particular state during sleep. The phenomena of OOB is as natural as you would term sleep to be natural, bearing in mind what I have said about the levels of sleep into which one can enter.

Many people who do not claim to have any psychic ability whatsoever can, nonetheless, give supportive evidence to their ability to project, at will, their astral counterpart from their physical body. I myself can do it. And, although it happens involuntarily to all people, I believe that the greater the need the body has to be re-charged, the further away from the physical counterpart the astral body travels.

Of course, we are not talking about physical distances. This psychic wilderness has no bearing on distance. If you like, you can imagine Dante's inferno as an example. Or perhaps your own concept of hell. While you are in a gross state of mind and existence, you cannot do anything else but enter into it, be you saint or sinner.

Once the astral body enters into a certain area, which can be known as deep sleep, we are virtually separated from our physical state. We are then in this psychic wilderness where everything is distorted and yet has an amazing clarity within your dream state. Yet, it has no sense of reality. As I have said, the people that you are with in this state may bear no relation to the people you know in the third-dimensional world. They have their own identities. But consider this. Millions of people are asleep at the same time. Millions of vibrations are also entering into this pulsating mass of energy and nobody can have a positive control over it. Even the trained adept can go nowhere without having to pass through this psychic wilderness.

Let us return to those who are in a coma. Do they dream? Have they entered into that same twilight world and are they experiencing what we experience in our dreams—but at a greater level of understanding? We are restricted, even in sleep, by the confines of our physical body. Is it not possible that those in a coma state are able to go far beyond, and that the dreams they have in this twilight world of reality are such that they do not disturb them, that they can experience all things, tap into all the other dreamers, tap into this flowing energy field? Is it not possible that they are indeed part of it, while they lie in their comatose state?

There are numerous cases and arguments that now reign as to whether or not we have the right to switch off the life-support machines of these people in a coma state. I realize I am not sufficiently qualified, in a medical sense, to enter this argument with any great or definite conviction. But my own personal opinion is that I don't think it matters whether we throw the life-support switch or not, although there is an argument that we should wait for some great scientific breakthrough to bring these people out of their coma. And this argument seems to be well founded. I personally believe, however, that these people are separate from their bodies. They are within that psychic force field and they have become part of their environment. The anxiety and pain is felt only by the family. It isn't felt by the victims—it cannot be felt by them because they are without emotion. They are experiencing the true reality of this energy field, which I maintain the psychic (and the psychic faculty) draws upon.

Those that study and practice the ancient arts, such as astrology, numerology, the runes, the tarot, auric readings, and so forth, which are all allied and come under the same wide umbrella, base their art on ancient formulas. They emphasize that these ancient formulas have been in existence since man first began to reason; to organize themselves into primitive societies. The witch doctors, the shamans, and the priests—why do they emphasize that the more ancient the formula, the more credibility it has? Why? Perhaps this is one of the reasons we, the psychic fraternity, have not progressed and why we are not achieving any major breakthrough in what we term psychic phenomena. Science is constantly expanding its frontiers, constantly looking for progress. Things that are taking place today would not have seemed possible twenty years ago. So, why don't we, the psychics, adopt a more modern outlook in relation to the world of the paranormal? Why have we not advanced also?

Scientifically, we know that our brains, as well as our physical stature and appearance, have developed more over the past 100 years—and our intelligence has increased. As a result of scientific discoveries, we have found that we cannot close the door to any possibility. But, those who argue the case for the medium, those who seek to avoid the possibility of advancement by failing to take personal responsibility for being "psychic," who seek to disguise it under the cloak of some external individual "being" that is controlling them, have done little to widen the barriers of the paranormal world.

At the beginning of the book, I used one of the most ancient reference sources—the first book of the Bible, Genesis. And most of the practitioners of what we term the ancient art of magic accept Genesis as being the most significant book of the Bible. But my interpretation is not meant to be taken as fact. It has simply been given as a focal point.

Scientists are constantly making new discoveries and are loudly proclaiming their latest findings. Society is being dictated to by science. Let me quote an example. Red wine, at one time, was considered dangerous to one's personal health. As soon as this research finding was published, people took notice and began to moderate their drinking habits. Within a very short period of time, however, science then backtracked and stated that the drinking of red wine was actually good for the heart.

The modern "fad" is to look after and improve the physical state of our bodies. We are advised to take up jogging and to get regular exercise, to try and achieve a balanced, possibly vegetarian or organic diet. We are advised to moderate our intake of alcohol and cigarettes. All these things are extremely important, particularly in a society as stressful as today's. But is it not possible that, at some later stage, scientific discoveries will force the scientists to turn around and maybe admit that too much exercise is bad for you? What do we do then? We constantly fluctuate. And, although science is, at all times, prepared to debunk its own theories as advancements are made, the practitioners of the psychic arts, to date, have not been prepared to debunk their own theories. This they must do. We are all psychic, and by now you should begin to understand what it is that I am saying. In other words, when you have finished reading this book, your psychic awareness should be greater, although you are not likely to go out and solve murders as a result of your newly discovered psychic ability.

Most people who knew me when I was active on the psychic scene and became known as "Britain's number one psychic detective" seem to carry a firm impression of an abrasive, blunt-speaking individual. I suppose it was true. I had my own vision of truth. I still have, and nothing will deter me from it. Looking back, sometimes with embarrassment at the way I arrogantly "strode through barriers," I now see the reason for it, and I realize it applies to each and every one of us. There must come a time when we reach a comparative level within our own conscience and therefore our actions are not decided or dictated by social niceties, are not dictated by what is considered to be "the norm," but are dictated by our own conscience.

Your awareness is there at all times, and as you tap into it, you begin to develop more and more. But there has to be a safety valve. That safety valve is your own conscience, that which knows what is truth. At the same time, we are still subjected to the normal human frailties of anger and the expression of it. And, as we have already indicated, it is important to be able to control it—once you have achieved psychic awareness—because of the adverse effect it can have, not only on others but on yourself.

My object is to provoke a reaction among you. If that reaction is one of absolute rejection, that is not good. Do not dismiss it. Analyze why you want to reject it. I put forward my beliefs and theories as a stimulus. By now you will have begun to achieve an opening-up and expansion of your mind. You are already beginning to enter into this psychic wilderness and you are able to tune in to specific things. Therefore, the more your mind can be prodded and provoked, the better.

One advantage I have is that, for the past seven

years, I have not taken part in any experiments concerning the psychic faculty. I virtually withdrew from the scene to be able to determine my own growth and, in doing so, I now realize that I must vigorously pursue my own investigations. There are no limits whatsoever, but each, in time, will achieve his or her own limitations.

chapter 8 Cultivating the Wilderness

Take a stroll on a clear, starlit night. Try to find a place where you can be completely alone with your thoughts. Look up into the night sky and consider the vastness of the universe, the Galaxy and galaxies beyond our own. It is almost impossible to begin to understand and penetrate the vastness of space, and one naturally looks for something tangible, an anchor.

For centuries, that anchor has been religion. It has been solid and it has held us fast and prevented movement. Now, as you develop your own personal awareness, you are able to look beyond "the norm." Try not to question or attempt to define, but observe and accept that this is you, and you are that.

When you next play your psychic development tape, go beyond the freedom of becoming that white horse and allow yourself to simply expand. Having crossed the barrier of the conscious and the subconscious, you can now ask yourself the questions: Can you not become, and have you not become, that vast universal space?

The removal of the illusionary circle places you in the center of existence. Let the scientists continue to advance technology, ultimately creating a better material life. Allow other people of different religions and philosophies to express themselves without hindrance. Do not be swayed or tempted to enter into discussion with them, hoping that you can convert them to your way of thinking. Concentrate solely upon achieving what you have already begun to achieve—the awareness of yourself and of the psychic faculty.

Remember the example of the circle; how vitally important it was to be able to recognize no-thing. By now you should be able to erase that illusionary circle without fear, confident in the knowledge of what you have achieved so far. Remember, the further you go, the more you develop, the more you will become aware of your own true self, of your own psychic faculty operating, of your own condemnation of your actions, realizing more and more the necessity for balance and harmony.

Throughout my early days in Spiritualism (in fact, from the very first time I was introduced to it), a medium informed me that I had with me a guide, a very large, black Zulu. He was, apparently, giving me strength. I also had an Egyptian guide, who was giving me wisdom. And, as I continued to visit Spiritualist centers all over Britain, my supposed guides became more numerous.

Those who claimed to be mediumistic and clairvoyant were constantly telling me that it was these guides who were using me, imparting through me their knowledge and truth. This constantly puzzled me because I was still feeling my way around. I wasn't sure what this truth was.

I needed no convincing of the continuation of man's existence. I was questioning the state of survival, not survival itself. Somehow, I could not accept the words of these mediums. I had to accept sole responsibility for what I said. Equally, I couldn't completely reject these mediums, who were able to see and perceive what was beyond the normal range of perception. However, it seemed they did not recognize themselves as simply "channels."

So it is odd that I, who for many years have been strongly against Spiritualism and its allegiance to guides, should now declare that I have found and accepted a personal guide. There is nothing grand about my personal guide. He isn't a big, strong, black Zulu, or a wise Egyptian. In fact, I have no concept of my guide being human at all. But I call him Jiminy Cricket. "He" is actually my conscience. It is constantly telling me what I do wrong. It is constantly causing me to think about what I have said and forces me to retract any harsh words or malevolent thoughts. It also makes me realize, more and more, the importance of being able to control myself and my emotions.

The energy one can release can be so damaging that it can have adverse effects on other people, but by channeling it in the right direction, it can have the most positive and beneficial effect of all—that of healing.

Healing is an expression of the psychic ability. I gave you the earlier example of the two plants. You should now be able to see and feel a difference, particularly when you charge the water. As you hold your hand above the glass and concentrate on pushing energy from the center of your palm into the water, you should begin to feel a slight heat emanating from your hand. You should begin to feel a resistance against your palm, as you project this psychic energy, the same energy that heals.

Perhaps the greatest healer today is Matthew Manning. As a young man, he was very much involved with the Spiritualist movement. I have watched his career from the time he was considered by the Spiritualist movement to be the greatest thing since Harry Edwards.

And Manning has grown and developed to such an extent that he doesn't need the Spiritualist label anymore. He has "found" himself and he is able to project his abilities in the most positive, beneficial way possible.

Interestingly, and I believe this enhances my theory regarding the psychic wilderness and the ability everyone has to tap into it, before Manning developed his healing abilities, honing them to a very fine degree, he dabbled in automatic writing and art, claiming the ability in both fields was transmitted through him by a dead person, or persons.

Manning was able to close his mind, pick up a pen and write, without any thought or consideration, about subjects of which he had no knowledge. Manning also produced pictures that were acclaimed by art critics as being the work of an advanced, trained artist. In the early days, he claimed the work was actually that of a dead artist who was controlling him.

I believe what was really happening to Manning was that he was somehow tapping into this psychic wilderness, where all things are, before he properly understood it, before he had properly begun to cultivate it. I believe I went through the same process in my youth. We were both reacting to this wilderness and struggling to find our way through it. My aim is to help you to be able to cultivate this wilderness.

A dictionary definition of "wilderness" is "desert, state of desolation or confusion." On side one of the psychic development tape, when you took your first steps into meditation, the symbolism was that of crossing the desert and, within that desert, coming to an oasis. Consider this symbolism as we now discuss the cultivation of that wilderness.

When we enter a darkened room, we automatically seek to turn on the light. When we do so, everything becomes clear and recognizable. We have dispersed the darkness and the gloom, and we are able to perceive, with absolute clarity, all that is good. Remember this imagery whenever you think about, or enter, the psychic wilderness. Concentrate on the chakra at the center of your forehead. Open it. Symbolize it as a beam of light that you can direct straight ahead of you, so that you can disperse the shadows and so that entering the wilderness will hold no fear for you, because you are able to see clearly what you are doing.

Always remember the importance of protecting your aura and closing down the chakras. If you do this, you will have nothing to fear.

I wonder what the scientific response is to the phenomenon known as child prodigies? For example, in the early nineteenth century, a five-year-old boy known as Benjamin Blyth asked his father at what hour was he born. His father replied: "4:00 p.m."

"What time is it now ?" asked Benjamin.

"7:50 p.m." replied the intrigued father.

Within a matter of seconds, Benjamin stunned his father by declaring: "I am now 188,352,000 seconds old."

The bemused father decided to work out his son's age, in seconds. After a while, he said to his son: "You seem to be out by 172,800 seconds. How did you calculate that number?"

Benjamin replied: "Don't forget the leap years."

Further calculation by his father proved Benjamin to be totally correct in his initial calculation.

I think little else was heard of Benjamin Blyth; nonetheless, this obscure event was recorded. But, from where did the boy obtain this knowledge? There are so many recorded instances of young children suddenly developing an ability to sit at a piano and, without any tuition whatsoever, begin to play a melody.

One answer to this could be that the ability comes from the nine-tenths of the brain that we believe lies dormant and about which we know very little. According to scientists, on average, we use about 10 percent of our total brain power. I believe the brain itself is a miniature universe. Science has been able to map part of this universe and can now specifically identify general areas of the brain that have a definite purpose, controlling specific limb movements and providing direct stimulation.

However, my question is: If we only use 10 percent of the brain, of what value is the other 90 percent? I believe that, ultimately, science will continue to plot the brain "universe" and identify, more accurately, the precise functions of specific parts of the brain. And I think it is reasonable to assume that parts of the dormant 90 percent do, in fact, have specific purposes. Only time and study will unlock these secrets. I further believe the answer to child prodigies suddenly developing abilities and talents for which they have received no formal training does not lie in the brain but in the psychic wilderness, and that children's minds, in particular, not yet closed and fettered by intellect or advanced reasoning, are open and able to wander freely into this wilderness without the child having any concept or understanding of what he or she is doing. It is almost as if they are finding little chinks, little avenues, into the psychic wilderness and, from it, they are receiving information, in a similar way to that in which a radio receives transmissions.

We have talked at great length about psychic shocks and of the inherent dangers of not protecting yourself when you first begin to enter into the psychic wilderness.

Would you consider putting your finger into a live electric socket, while at the same time standing in a bucket of water? Or play Russian roulette? The vast majority of us would say "no!" Yet far too many people

involve themselves in something much more dangerous. They play with a Ouija board.

This might seem innocuous enough. The letters of
the alphabet are placed in a circle, with the words
"Yes" and "No" prominently placed in the center. The
object of the so-called game is for a group of people to
place their index fingers on an upturned glass or the
planchette placed in the center of the circle of letters
and wait for the glass to move toward individual letters
in the hope that it will spell out specific words, in the
form of a message.

An observer, who is not involved in the circle of people, is chosen to write down each letter to which the
glass travels.

Some commercial companies even market the Ouija
board as a game, with no warning or explanation as to
the potential dangers. The word "Ouija" comes from
the French and German words for "yes." There is no
mention of the more important word—"no."

As your awareness develops, you will recognize, for
yourself, the absolute stupidity and danger of playing
this psychic roulette. But, just as a child prodigy finds
cracks in the psychic wilderness, think of the effect
that can be achieved if several people direct their energy toward these cracks.

It takes only one susceptible, perceptive mind to receive a burst of energy from one of the cracks in the
psychic wilderness to influence the whole procedure
when a group dabbles with the Ouija board. That one
person could possibly be suffering from some minor
psychological disorder that creates unstable vibrations
and, once joined with the energy pouring through the
psychic wilderness crack, that will create a powerful
negative force. Like attracts like.

There are far too many documented cases of people
who have dabbled with this energy while playing with

the Ouija board, people desperate to contact those they love who have passed away, because it is believed they will be able to communicate through the Ouija board.

On a number of occasions, these vulnerable people have left with very disturbed minds, having received strange messages purporting to be from their deceased love ones. Messages received through the Ouija board have claimed that the place where their loved ones now reside is wonderful, that they are glad that they are no longer in the physical state and actually encourage their distraught relatives or friends to join them. As a result, some particularly vulnerable or disturbed people have committed suicide.

I know of people who claim to be psychic and have attempted to influence others by giving them messages and readings. They place total reliance on the Ouija board and its messages, citing the "fact" that every time they "play" with the board, they are able to communicate with the same personality who imparts wonderful new knowledge and has directed them to relay a message to another person.

As a result, the recipients of such messages change their whole approach to life, accepting that they are receiving direct communication from a higher spirit that has far greater knowledge than they do. This is absolutely ridiculous, as well as being highly dangerous.

At its weakest, energy leaking from the psychic wilderness can be likened to a mischievous child. At its strongest, it is totally malevolent and uncontrollable. One analogy that comes to mind is trying to stem a raging torrent of water by placing a small boulder in its path. I wrote about one particular demonstration of this force in my first book, *Clues to the Unknown*, where I intervened when a group of people were recklessly playing with a Ouija board. I was physically pinned to a wall by a levitating table, before I was able to use my experience in such matters. I eventually resisted this negative force and managed to release myself from its grip, an unnerving situation.

Be warned. The Ouija board, like poltergeist activities, if left uncontrolled, can eventually have the same devastating effect by taking control of a weakness. Wherever you find chinks in the wilderness that leak energy, that same energy is seeking chinks in a person's individual psychological makeup. And when such chinks are found, the energy can create total havoc, leading to possession and obsession, where even the most skilled psychiatrist can find no answer and must ultimately do battle with an energy that does not conform to any known scientific norm.

Mental institutions are full of unfortunate individuals suffering from split personality, delusions of hearing voices, and multiple personalities. The majority of these people have probably never come into contact with a Ouija board, but I believe that the negative energy leaking from the psychic wilderness has found the chinks in their individual psychological makeup and I strongly believe that a possible solution could be to treat them with psychic healing, which is positive and can counterbalance the negative energy leak that is affecting them.

I believe also that poltergeist activity can be firmly laid at the door of these chinks in the wilderness. Poltergeist activity is accepted as being excess energy emanating from certain individuals, commonly associated with adolescent children. In the main, these children are able to subconsciously control a great deal of the activity. I believe that they have tapped in to the psychic wilderness and the energy that is manifesting from them is having an adverse effect on the immediate environment and objects.

Contrary to the opinion of some, it is not the work of

individual entities that no longer exist in the physical world. It is simply an uncontrollable burst of energy. Once again, I must strongly emphasize the need for individuals to be able to control this energy and not let it run amok.

We have touched on the subject of psychic healing. Now let us expand on that. The first experiment, involving the plants, should now begin to show results. You should practice the charging of water each and every day. The more time you have spent meditating with the help of the psychic development tape, the more you should be able to feel and recognize this positive power within you—and you should be able to direct it anywhere that you wish, in a positive manner; in other words, you should able to project pure energy.

When you are feeling low and need some form of energy boost, simply concentrate on your breathing, slowly advancing it to a point where you begin to recognize the life force of which you are part and that is all around you.

Now, begin to enhance your breathing and concentrate as you breathe in deeply. Hold it in and be aware that, as you do so, you are charging yourself with this energy. Feel it. The more you breathe in, the clearer your mind will become and the more energy you will possess.

Your own body will dictate the need to charge itself while you are in a low energy state. Retain this energy. Do not discharge it in any other direction than within or it will only leave you depleted. However, when you are in a positive state of mind, when you are feeling good and are able to express and use this energy, do so in the most positive manner by directing it toward a person in need or an atmosphere that needs lifting.

Remember, it is vitally important after such an exercise to close down your chakras and enclose your aura, thus preventing anything of an adverse nature coming back toward you. Always protect yourself in this manner, as covered in the exercise on side two of the psychic development tape. Remember when you heard that sharp "crack," which disturbed your aura, and everything about you jangled? Now you will begin to understand this and to realize how essential it is to protect yourself at all times.

For centuries, most religions have maintained the belief in the positive power of prayer and that the more people involved in the act of prayer, the stronger the positive energy will become. This energy is not necessarily being projected in one specific direction but into the wilderness as a whole, where it will encompass all, in the same way that switching on the light in a dark room will illuminate everything within that room.

Instead of talking about prayer, substitute the word "healing," the projection of psychic power. Consider the fate of those who lie in a coma. Logic tells us that medical science is unable to do anything. So why, therefore, should we be able to help them? Who knows what boundaries we can cross? People do come out of this state many times as a result of somebody speaking to them repeatedly or playing a favorite piece of music. In the same way, when you are directing energy it is being sent in a positive manner—to reach into this wilderness and for the person to be able to respond. There have been miraculous recoveries as a result of this. But do not concern yourself if you don't achieve miraculous results. The psychic wilderness contains all conditions and those in a comatose state are caught up there with millions of other vibrations and thoughts, negative as well as positive, in a swirling morass of energy.

Think of a very simple experiment you probably performed at school when you studied science. Do you remember throwing iron filings onto a sheet of paper and, by placing a magnet underneath the paper and drawing it in one direction, you transformed the iron filings from their jumbled mass into a clearly defined magnetic field?

Your mind can be this magnet and you can channel it to your hand. As you direct the energy into the water for your plant experiment, visualize a definite pattern emerging.

This wilderness must ultimately be cultivated so that it becomes as natural a part of our existence as the physical state. The more you accept it and recognize it now, and the more you fill it with positive thoughts, the more you begin to straighten and cultivate it. By relating yourself to the magnet, the more positive you become and the greater the achievement. After involving yourself in directing energy, close down your chakras and enclose your aura. If you protect yourself at all times, you are able to recharge yourself and to take in this energy consciously, so that your mind begins to balance itself with the physical body.

Sleep is most beneficial. Your attitude toward sleep must be that you need it to charge yourself. To be able to prepare yourself for sleep, bypassing the lower levels of negative confusion that can create bad dreams, spend some time concentrating on your breathing and on the center of your forehead.

You will find that this is a wonderful cure for insomnia. Simply by concentrating and relaxing in the most positive manner, you will enter into sleep naturally and there will be no awareness of passing through this wilderness. You have prepared yourself. You are your own beacon of light and this will take you in the correct direction, being recharged in a field of positive energy. Remember also that, symbolically, the chakra of your forehead represents a torch whose light will pass through this wilderness. It will encompass and lighten the immediate area around you in the most positive way. So, imagine this light magnified a million times by a million other minds—creating the same positive effect. And remember, the smallest candle will illuminate the darkest room.

As I stated in *Clues to the Unknown*, I think there is somebody who could be placed on a par with Matthew Manning, if not greater, somebody who chooses not to use his energy in that direction. That man is Uri Geller. Geller prefers to remain a "showman," using a unique ability that very few people have to produce a very definite effect on solid metal objects.

I sometimes wonder if this is how history will remember Uri Geller—as a "showman," a cabaret act, a spoon-bender. Or will he be remembered for advancing the frontiers of the paranormal—for making a unique contribution to our understanding of psychic healing? Think of the greater benefit he could impart by using that energy as Matthew Manning does, projecting healing power to its greatest effect.

And you can develop this ability in the same way, as you develop your awareness of vibrations and as your perception becomes keener; as you become more aware of your environment and the subtle changes that can take place, you too can become aware of this energy field. It is there to be used, to heal.

Manning has had remarkable recorded successes in removing cancerous growths as a result of his projecting psychic energy through his hands. We cannot all be Matthew Mannings, as we cannot all be Uri Gellers. Each one of us is individual and unique. But we can all use this healing energy for the benefit of others, even though they might be totally unaware of what we are doing. For example, you may be sitting in a room with somebody and become aware of the tangled vibrations that are emanating from that person. You can sense that they are uneasy, unable to relax. Project energy toward them, the same energy that you experience within your meditation. Observe the effect it can have.

One word of caution here. Be careful how you use this energy, for although used correctly, it can calm a person, incorrect use can agitate that person. The responsibility is yours alone.

You will not achieve this overnight; it is a gradual process. But you are on your way to achieving it and you will eventually do so. This book is not going to give you all the answers; neither is it going to help you realize your full potential. It will be through your own efforts that you do so. I am simply showing you the way. How far you go is dependent on you. But you can do it. It is that simple.

How many times have you become angry with someone and isolated yourself with your anger? You will know the effect it can have on you. It remains with you and it is difficult to shake off. Another psychic would see a black cloud over your head, created by your mood. But you can disperse it by raising your concentration from the solar plexus to the center of your forehead and from there to the top dead-center of your head.

Expand yourself as if you are mentally blowing away this black cloud. You can do this in a positive way. But should you project it in a negative way to somebody who is unaware of his or her psychic ability, that person will be adversely affected.

In the olden days, witches played a very important part in medieval society and were considered to be very powerful people. It was believed that witches were able to project thoughts and energies and cast harmful spells. Is it not possible that, rather than casting spells, they simply were aware of their psychic energy and were projecting it in a negative way—to create an adverse effect on those they wished to harm?

In developing our awareness, we are able to use this energy in one positive direction. Our minds can create whatever we choose. I would rather that we concentrate on what we do not know—what our subconscious mind will present for us to be able to recognize it. That is far more important and has more value. This is why we continue to find our inner awareness—to break through the barrier between the conscious and subconscious and awaken the psychic faculty.

The true clairvoyant is considered to be able to see our past, our present, and our future. A clever psychologist can tell us about our past. By allowing us to speak, he can come to understand our type of personality and can take a fair guess as to our background. He may even pinpoint accurately a specific event that has caused our present condition.

Similarly, the clairvoyant, having spent some time in your presence, can accurately "home in" on certain past events. The clairvoyant may well pick up your present state and this can be confirmed or denied. When it comes to the future, however, we have to be extremely careful, because the future is determined by what takes place now.

With a fair understanding of a person's psychological makeup, it is relatively easy to anticipate an event that is likely to happen to that individual. I am not contradicting my earlier statement, where I said one can foresee major events that are not necessarily affecting individuals but a complete area. I am simply saying that one can foresee an event that may take place as far as the individual is concerned, but can predict the outcome only as a result of understanding that person's psychological makeup, that is, how he or she would react in certain situations.

It is not my intention to offend anybody on this issue. So let me clarify my point. Spiritualism, and the people involved within the movement, was instrumental in helping me to comprehend more fully the psychic faculty. It is true to say that I developed my psychic faculty under the guidance of those to whom I gave credit as having a greater knowledge. Unfortunately, they also showed me an aspect that I could not fully accept. I believe, strongly, that the ability to see and recognize what is beyond the range of normal perception should be of greater importance and should have a greater impact upon our lives. Yet it would appear that some Spiritualists are focusing their energies not on helping people achieve their own awareness but on setting themselves up as counselors, being in a position to determine the future for those who seek help through private consultations. On occasions, I feel they skate on thin ice by attempting to diagnosis a medical condition. I have heard mediums and psychics tell people publicly that the condition affecting them physically was other than that diagnosed by their doctors. They have then gone on to advocate an alternative method of treatment. This I felt was dangerous and I still do.

In the main, I found that people who sought the guidance and advice of mediums were in an extremely emotional and vulnerable state, particularly those who had lost somebody close. They would clutch at any straw, so they naturally turned toward these mediums to fill the gap in their lives left by the death of their loved ones.

I felt it was important for them to receive confirmation of survival, or some indication that their loved ones still existed in spirit. But when it was taken further and the vulnerable recipients of the message were told what they should do with their lives (rather than allow them to think for themselves), I felt the mediums were assuming too much responsibility. I will constantly reiterate that the responsibility is yours—and yours alone. These are your inherent abilities—to develop, to analyze, to understand and to control. But before we can control it we have to accept that it exists.

In effect, all things exist. Perhaps then we can begin to have more understanding of the Spiritualist within this theory of the wilderness. Every aspect of what has been experienced remains—music, art, thoughts, impressions. Everything lingers. It cannot disappear. And survival after death becomes a little more understandable if we forget about the stages of life and death and just concentrate on all that is; all that has been developed as a result of early pioneers; all the wonderful music that remains within this energy field. It remains within this wilderness—and that is why we must cultivate it.

Who knows what else remains hidden, waiting to be discovered, or even rediscovered? This possibility excites me enormously and, in rediscovering it, will it enable us to go much further than before, hand in hand with science, to push back the boundaries of our scientific and psychic knowledge for the benefit of all mankind? By accepting the premise that everything remains in existence, we can also begin to understand telepathy. To a certain degree, many people telepathically receive vibrations emanating from this wilderness, and we also know that telepathic communication between individuals is a reality. So, is there a connection? Of course there is.

We have conducted the experiment where we select an individual whilst using public transport and try to feel and understand his or her personality. Now let us take the experiment a stage further.

The next time you use public transport, and you have time to spare, select a fellow passenger and, by bringing the whole of your concentration to the center of your forehead, mentally call them, to make them turn and face you. Feel the puzzlement they experience as they do so. Perhaps the best example (which should cause you some amusement) is to sit behind a person and mentally "tickle" the back of their ears or neck.

After a while, you will see the person begin to twitch, maybe even scratch the back of their head. This exercise is harmless, of course, but it is once again enabling you to prove to yourself the ability you have developed.

Once you have tickled their neck, go one step further. Try to make them turn around. They are feeling slightly uncomfortable. They are feeling this pure energy that you are directing toward them, but because they don't know what it is, it unsettles them slightly and they may feel a little uncomfortable. Eventually, they will turn around. Once you have achieved this, cease your projections and send out a simple beam of light toward them to enable them to feel settled and at ease once again.

The object of the exercise is for you to be able to prove to yourself the ability you have developed and to be able to direct it in simple experiments such as this. As you develop, you should find that you are able to communicate telepathically.

Think of a friend with whom you wish to communicate. Concentrate on that person and impel them to pick up the telephone and call you. Try it and you will be amazed at the results.

All these exercises should indicate to you that you are able to project and use psychic energy. The next thing you should try is dowsing. This is something completely different to anything you have attempted before. Dowsing is a natural phenomena and no training seems to be necessary to accomplish this. Neither is it necessary to be aware of your psychic energy. I believe that more than 60 percent of the population can dowse.

So, what is the best way for you to practice this and prove to yourself that you can dowse? You have become aware of your abilities and you are beginning to see the psychic energy at work. This should benefit you even more.

Try this. Take two metal coat hangers from your closet. Bend each of them so that one straight side is between ten to twelve inches, and the other, at a right angle, is about five inches long.

Hold them in your hands, as shown below:

Concentrate on being able to hold these two pieces of wire without any movement in a way that prevents you from controlling their movement, using the natural folds of your hands.

Sit comfortably and with your arms held out, about one foot apart from each other, point the dowsing rods in a forward direction, as illustrated. Now, concentrating on either rod, try to move it inwardly, toward you. Then, try it with the second. And, with patience, you will succeed in achieving results.

Assume the same starting position, and now try to make the dowsing rods move away from each other. Spend time practicing this, and then try bringing one toward you and the other pointing in an outward direction. You will be amazed at the results, and the more you practice, the more fun you will have. It is an amusing and completely harmless experiment.

Could this be the beginning of developing telekinesis? Science, without any controlled experiment, would not even consider the possibility of there being any telekinetic ability there. But it is within your powers and for you to practice.

Taking the dowsing experiment a stage further, find yourself a reasonably large open area. Now, take six small, identical containers of the same size (tin cans or jars will do) and fill three of them with water, placing lids on all six so that the water is concealed. Ask your partner or friend to place these containers at various spots around the practice area.

Holding the dowsing rods as described, walk steadily forward in the direction of the first container. If it contains water, the dowsing rods should move inwards, toward each other, and cross over. Try it with all six containers and see what your success rate is. I promise you will be amazed at the results.

You can devise your own experiments. Ask somebody to bury a large bowl of water somewhere in an outside area. All you need to do is walk around the area and your dowsing rods will cross when you pass over the container of water.

Having explained this experiment, it is somewhat frustrating not to be able to give a satisfactory explanation as to why dowsing rods work. The more aware one is of psychic energy, the more positive the results. This I do know.

It occurs to me that perhaps this is a field where the

scientist and the psychic can work together and can co-operate with each other in pushing back the frontiers of our knowledge. I have already warned about the dangers of energy leaking from the psychic wilderness, whether through uncontrolled dabbling with the wilderness or by the intentional or unintentional punching of holes, chinks in the wilderness. The end result is the same. Energy leaks from the psychic wilderness and flows into our third-dimensional world. Is it possible then, by using an adapted version of dowsing (whereby the psychic adept does not come into physical contact with the rods, which are linked to scientific monitoring machines), for the scientist and the psychic together to be able to locate sources of energy leakage from the psychic wilderness?

On the one hand, the benefit of the psychic's involvement would be to close down the hole from which energy is leaking—to plug the flow of uncontrolled energy, which may be having an extremely adverse effect on psychically untrained individuals.

And, on the other hand, the scientist, because his monitoring machines tell him something is there, and because the machines register some source of power, can then formulate a hypothesis and can begin to investigate it further. Scientists accept that unseen power phenomena like gravity, magnetic fields, and wave bands of radiation do exist, because they have been able to measure them. So, I publicly challenge the scientific community to work hand in hand with the psychic adepts, to establish the existence of the psychic wilderness, and in doing so to expand our frontiers of knowledge.

chapter 9 The Physical Wilderness

Having become aware of the psychic wilderness, we are now slowly learning to cultivate it and to reap the benefits. Increasing familiarity and contact with this strange, even exciting, new environment, where all things are, may lead us to believe that a bright new future is opening up for us, a golden age where those psychic wilderness explorers hunt out the hidden treasures that are there waiting to be discovered and rediscovered.

A bright new future is opening up before us. But we cannot turn our backs on the past or on the present. To coin a phrase, our heads may be in the clouds, but our feet must remain firmly on the ground. There can be no bright new tomorrow for us if we attempt to bypass those who have nothing and those who struggle desperately just to survive the "physical wilderness." We cannot have our heads in the clouds if our feet crush those beneath us. We must learn to cultivate this physical wilderness. This is as essential as is our need to cultivate the psychic wilderness.

Perhaps the only example I can give here is what we were taught as children. Let us look at it, though, without any spiritual significance whatsoever. The story concerns Jesus, when he was said to have entered the wilderness for forty days and forty nights and was tempted by the Devil, who took Jesus to the highest point, where he could survey all the kingdoms of the world in a moment of time, and said: "To you I will give all this authority and their glory; for it has been delivered to me, and I give it to whom I will. If you then, will worship me, it shall all be yours." (Luke 4:6–8)

According to the Biblical story, Jesus rejected this offer. But does this offer not apply to us as well? We have learned to read and to analyze and to find our own concept of truth in all that is said and written. Can we now accept that the parable of Jesus's temptation in the wilderness is simply that of a man who becomes aware of the true potential within himself, struggling with his own conscience, because after being comparatively unaware for many years, he suddenly found everything he was searching for was within himself and, like others, found tremendous difficulty in accepting it?

He knew he had the ability and then became aware, not through the insistence of the Devil, but through his own conscience, which then tempted him. His own awareness caused him to realize that, through his abilities, he could have all the material benefits he wanted. There was nothing to prevent him from achieving this except his own conscience, which he battled with in the wilderness. Dismiss all those material possessions and what is not important to achieve your own goal. In other words, the symbolism of Jesus in the wilderness is that of a man desperately trying to come to terms with himself in an attempt to sublimate the egotistical drive that is so essential but that needs to reach a perfect balance.

Have we not also experienced these situations in modern-day life? Those people who set themselves up as spiritual teachers or gurus, those who make claims and insist on creating a following. By having a following, does not the guru receive adulation and recognition as being something extraordinary and separate from other people? Why do we continue to insist, when by now we should be aware that it is one's self, only the individual self, that can establish and find truth.

We cannot just solely cultivate the psychic wilderness; we must also balance it with our understanding of our own physical existence and become aware of all those that do not have the ability or the opportunity to investigate or achieve awareness.

Therefore, the responsibility must be yours—not necessarily to preach to the converted but to become aware of all that is around you, all that is within you. You should not seek to separate yourself from the physical wilderness and from those caught up in its seemingly inescapable thickets. You should make the effort to reach out and embrace such people; you should not reject them. In rejecting them and their predicament, you reject a necessary part of yourself, and your search for awareness will have no grounding.

Consider the predicament of the prostitute. We are all aware of this type of woman and her style of dress, provocative in its extreme. We are aware that she is willing to sell her body and there are those among us who are only too happy to avail themselves of her services.

But, is she a prostitute or is she a person? What causes her to become a prostitute? Your own psychic awareness and abilities should enable you to be able to look a little closer and to see the loneliness, the deprivation, that has probably caused her to enter into this direction.

Perhaps there are puncture marks on her arms, showing that she has fallen victim to drug abuse, having been introduced to it by somebody else, maybe her pimp who encouraged her into prostitution in the first place. What is it that has caused her to reach this point?

There are also prostitutes who, without using drugs or experiencing deprivation, view what they are doing quite simply as a means of earning money and having the good things in life, the material things. Is it not possible that this particular type of prostitute has listened to her devil in the wilderness and has decided to take on board all that was offered to her—material benefits, material gains—without concern for anyone else?

Regardless of what category they fall into, are these prostitutes not part of us, the human family? And are we not part of them? But we reject them. We find them and their lifestyle distasteful. Having stated previously that you can recognize nothing that does not exist, if you recognize distrust or distaste (even lust), it is because it is within you.

The prostitute, in seeking you, as the customer, to avail yourself of her services, according to sociological investigation, is able to close down her personality and her feelings. In pursuing this action on a regular basis, what have they lost? Will they be able to give themselves to a true, meaningful relationship afterward? Is this, in fact, what they are desperately seeking? Many will not want to be converted back to a life of normality, as we would term it, but that does not mean we should dismiss them. We cannot dismiss them, because we are still looking to create a future of understanding between all people. Having achieved your awareness, you cannot dismiss such people. You must accept and embrace them as being an essential part of your growth thus far.

There is another modern phenomena I would like you to consider, one that I personally experienced thirty years ago, that of being down and out, homeless, not knowing where my next meal was coming from. It is a sad reflection on society today that this tragic situation still exists. In fact, we recognize that it is even worse today than it was thirty years ago. You cannot walk around any major city in Britain today without being approached by someone who is down and out, begging for the price of a cup of coffee. Some even give you the impression that they expect, as their right, that you should give money to them.

It could be that you have shielded yourself against it for so long that you don't even recognize the fact that it probably happens to you every single day. You could be going about your everyday business, hurrying to or from work, shopping, or enjoying some leisure time. Then, walking along a street, you notice a person whom you believe to be a tramp, a homeless person, a beggar. You realize that in a few more paces your paths will cross. Perhaps you even have a flash of thought, wondering whether you can cross the road to avoid your paths crossing, but you cannot. As you approach the person, his hand stretches out and he begs for money to buy a cup of coffee, to buy food. How many of you hurry on past these people without even acknowledging their existence, without even looking at them?

As you turn your back on them, they abuse you, they curse you, but you walk on regardless. What has happened here? What has taken place during this interaction between two human beings?

Most of them will sarcastically turn around and say: "Have a nice day." But think about the one that is desperate, craving an alcoholic drink. They can't control this craving. It is a very serious addiction. If you give them money, they are either going to say: "Thank you very much, God bless you," or make some reference to your meanness. And, when they abuse you, it is out of pure frustration and in effect like a bolt of energy that they throw at you; and it hits you, and you don't know how to react.

Are you going to react by saying: "How dare you?" In many instances, it is virtually impossible for them to get out of the rut—the problem is now too great. But, you want to turn around and say: "How dare you? I earn my money, and you sit there expecting it to be given to you." But, he has "hit" you. He has affected you. And it is very difficult to just walk away after receiving this insult. It is something that you can't ward off.

This expression of anger, this projection of energy also affects the beggar. When the next customer comes along, the beggar will try hard to beg for money, but in actual fact his anger is still there. He is seething. And, after a while, he finds it impossible to beg for money. His attitude becomes very hostile and he may well decide to steal money or rob the next passerby.

The beggar, day by day, is building up his internal anger and tension and isolating himself further from this society that he believes is rejecting him. So he, in turn, rejects society, sometimes quite violently. In doing so, he is attracting, through the chinks in the psychic wilderness, negative oppressive anger. It will be channeled back through him because like attracts like, and there is a perfect open channel for it. The moment you turn on the tap, the energy is just going to gush out. And so, you are getting this interaction, and to a certain degree he is becoming a channel with this expression of anger. And it is all around him. This is a very dangerous situation for everyone, and it should, and must, concern us.

I am not advocating that every time someone asks for money, you should oblige. This is an impossibility, a drain on your own limited resources, and very few people are able to do so.

It is also extremely difficult for you not to react to the abuse hurled at you. You have yet to achieve that which is virtually impossible within your physical state of being able to have complete love and understanding for your fellow man. Let us not try to confuse ourselves and pretend.

You will express anger, but providing you can immediately recognize your expression of anger and the reason you have expressed it, you are still learning. This is because, perhaps in the physical wilderness, the learning curve is even greater than that of the psychic wilderness. Here, you are faced with every day-to-day reality. You are subjected to the pressures and conditions of a material existence every day. And it is virtually impossible to walk about in a state of heightened awareness without this affecting you.

You are human and the years of conditioning cannot just be removed simply because you have entered into the psychic wilderness and have become aware of your psychic abilities. It does not make you superhuman. You will still get angry. You will still feel all the human emotions. All that we are saying here is: try to constantly be aware of it, not to ignore it.

If anything, with your heightened state of awareness, you are now more vulnerable to emotions—your own and those of other people. And, if other people are aware of this, they know that they can wound you far easier by saying that you have this awareness and yet it doesn't work very well.

It has often been written that I am myself a sensitive individual. And I think it is fair to say that as I developed my own awareness over many years, I did become more sensitive to what other people were feeling and therefore this is one of the reasons that I continue to stress that you should use the ability to protect yourself and to close down your chakras.

Throughout the book, I have used references from the Bible pertaining to one man to try to illustrate a point and at the same time to interpret what was alleged to have been said in keeping with your own development. I will use another.

It was when Jesus was being cross-examined by the Pharisees (Matthew 22:15–22) and they tried to trap him into saying that he was the son of God. Jesus asked for a coin and asked them whose head was on the coin.

They replied: "Caesar's."

Jesus then said: "Render therefore to Caesar the things that are Caesar's, and to God the things that are God's."

In other words, man has to live within the two worlds and man has to be quite clear about it. The two existences are not interchangeable and you must be clear as to which existence you are currently in and be aware of its constraints.

I believe there will be a natural revolution of awareness, as opposed to a natural revolution of violence. This will ultimately return us to the state of perfection. We cannot envisage it because of our concept of time. But time doesn't exist, so perfection is there and the fact that we can recognize it means that we can make progress toward it.

Providing we can live with our feet firmly placed in both worlds, we will be able to have a positive effect on those immediately around us, and the more people that become aware, the greater the effect.

One recent example of this comes to mind. I visited London recently for the first time in nearly six years. I had been living in Cyprus and had become used to the slower, less complex pace of life. So it came as something of a shock to me when I used the London Underground transport system.

I suddenly found people hurtling toward me, and I was surrounded by this intense, concentrated mass of energy. I could feel every possible vibration as this shifting mass of people went about their daily lives. I just couldn't stand this tremendous burst of energy and decided to get off at the next stop—to have a coffee and refocus myself.

I was familiar with the London "buzz," but I would say that the energy level had increased a thousandfold in just a few years.

Although I had an appointment to keep, I could afford to be a little late, and I reasoned that I needed to be relatively calm for my meeting. But, being caught up in this swirling, intense energy made that virtually impossible, and I was able to physically withdraw from it. Unfortunately, most people don't have that luxury. They have got to be on the train and they don't have the option of getting off—but they do have the opportunity to mentally withdraw from it for a few moments, and to analyze it and themselves; to calm themselves down. To find an oasis of peace within themselves.

This anecdote reminds me of the tale of the "mugging clip." During my time as a professional investigator, I was in New York on business and decided to walk to my meeting across Central Park. The work that I was involved in at the time presented dangers on a daily basis, so the mugger's paradise of Central Park felt like a normal, everyday environment to me. I was part of it and I was able to go out against it.

When I met my friends and told them I had walked across the park, they were shocked and more than a little concerned for my welfare. I suddenly realized that these people walked about in a state of permanent fear; so much so that they told me about the mugging clip.

Vendors were selling mugging clips, which people would put in their top pockets, with a $10 bill attached to it. If a mugger demanded money, the victim would take out the clip, and give it to the mugger, who would be in so much of a hurry that he would take it and run off—a possibly violent crime reduced to a brief and relatively inexpensive commercialized transaction.

At the time, I laughed about it but when I visited London after six years in Cyprus and walked into this field of energy, I suddenly appreciated what these people in New York were talking about.

The familiar imagery of a Victorian novel with its "danger lurking in every gas-lit alley" comes to mind very vividly for me. This imagery is very much alive today in the major cities of the world—and you can feel it. It has been created, and the energy is there, like a big black bowl.

You have to live within this environment and, in living within it, you have the problem of people who expect too much from you. They forget that you are human. You cannot be psychic twenty-four hours a day. You have to protect yourself. You have to close down the chakras.

And, if you have had a very bad day in the physical wilderness and arrive home somewhat confused and emotional, don't try to use your psychic development tape without the correct and proper preparation. You are not living on a desert island. You are very much part of the physical environment. You may even enter into a similarly bad environment when you arrive home, and if the time isn't right and you are not properly prepared, you will achieve no benefit from the psychic development tape.

Furthermore, if you are unable to blow this black cloud away, it is the wrong approach to believe you can escape into the psychic wilderness. You are not going to escape from anything. When you enter the psychic wilderness, it is to explore and learn, not to escape from the physical wilderness.

Living within the physical wilderness, you are better off listening to some relaxing music and having a few glasses of wine to help you relax.

It is always possible that, in the pursuit of personal awareness, you can run the risk of alienating your partner. Striving to achieve psychic awareness can cause resentment, because you can leave your partner behind. Your partner may not have your total commitment to the pursuit of awareness and may see your increased awareness as something separate, a threat. It becomes a third part of the relationship; the enemy within. Your partner is not getting your undivided attention. But, are you to be responsible for the emotions of someone else? This is a tricky question. You can attempt to explain what it is you are doing. And, to a certain extent, upon the partner with the greater awareness rests the greater responsibility to show the other what is actually being gained.

But, be warned. Pursuing psychic awareness to weld a relationship together will never work. This is the difficulty. If a relationship has reached a point where there seems to be no reconciliation possible, then there is nothing wrong whatsoever in being able to analyze it and look at it, because only you know the truth of the situation. Withdraw from it for a period or end it. Remaining in a bad relationship can only lead to problems.

It is difficult to come from a pressured work situation into a pressured domestic situation without reacting. But if you understand the need to retire and to reach a certain equilibrium, that is half the battle won.

Of course, other people may be involved if there is conflict between partners, because the physical environment children grow up in can become an emotional minefield. Children are very sensitive to vibrations and atmospheres, and if their parents are arguing and shouting, the child also enters into this confusion.

Parents are responsible for a child's physical, mental, and psychological growth. You should try to treat the child in your home as a guest. The child doesn't belong to you, the child belongs to mankind.

I cannot help but wonder whether some of the horrific crimes we read about that are committed by adults are the result of a trauma or even a mild emotional setback that the offender suffered as a child. Does a dominant but normally absent father, who settles an argument with his wife by shouting, psychologically encourage his child to believe that dominant, argumentative behavior in the playground is the correct way of going about things? Might is right.

Or does a subservient mother who can only get her way with her husband through stealth and woman's wiles encourage her child to use the same devious ploys at school? Children are great observers of life and, if they see something working and achieving a result, they will try it for themselves.

What are the current generation of parents teaching their children today, or have they absolved all responsibility for their children? Children are subjected to images of successful violence in feature films, television programs and, most worryingly, computer games, where the "goodies" achieve success by killing the "baddies" in the most vicious and violent ways possible.

A child actually feels a glow of success, of peer group approval, and even parental approval, if he can "kill" successfully. What messages are today's parents teaching their children, and will these lessons come back to haunt society in the future?

I believe very strongly that at some time in the adult life of a maladjusted and dysfunctional child that some leak in the psychic wilderness will find this person, enter through the cracks in his or her psychological makeup, and transport this person back into the mayhem of the video game. For this person, death and destruction will be a game. For society, it will be deadly serious.

If you want to achieve an ideal equilibrium for yourself as an individual, then find yourself a little island, sit there, and become at peace and at one with nature. But, of what value is this? You are achieving nothing, only self-gratification.

Achieving psychic awareness in itself doesn't mean that you become a balanced person. It can have the opposite effect. Therefore, you must strive to learn how to balance it with an understanding and awareness of the physical wilderness. There must be equilibrium between the two. There must be the necessary duality, if you are to take your journey onwards to greater heights.

I will end with a little story that encapsulates what I am trying to convey. It involved a very successful businessman named Mr. Brown. Unfortunately, as a result of the pressures of his business, Mr. Brown's marriage failed and he got divorced. After a time, he began to think that he had lost everything and was achieving nothing.

So, he bought a tumble-down cottage that was completely derelict, and it stood in a half acre of wilderness. He bought himself a little trailer, put it on the land, and settled down to rebuilding this cottage all by himself.

After a couple of weeks, the local village priest came to visit him and to welcome him to the village. The priest hoped he would see Mr. Brown in church the next Sunday. Mr. Brown said: "I'm not sure about that. You can see, I have a lot to do here."

A year passed by and the priest decided it was time to make another attempt to bring this wayward sheep back into the flock, so he again visited Mr. Brown. The priest couldn't believe the transformation that had taken place. The house was a picture and the half acre of wilderness had been transformed into a beautiful garden with flowers, trees, an immaculate lawn, a fish-pond and a fountain.

The priest saw Mr. Brown sitting in a chair under an umbrella, enjoying a glass of beer.

The priest said: "Oh, Mr. Brown. What a transformation. What an inspiration. Isn't it wonderful what we and God can do together?"

Mr. Brown turned, looked at the priest and said: "I'm not too sure about that. He had it on his own for a number of years and he didn't do a lot, did he?"

chapter 10 Endpoint: Merging with the Light

I have often stated that I know what I can do, but I do not know what I cannot do. One reason for this may be because what can be achieved is limitless. The possibilities are endless and even if one spent their entire human existence in the pursuit of greater awareness, one still might only garner a fraction of the knowledge, a fraction of the total awareness available.

Of course, one could quite reasonably ask: "Do we need to have total awareness? Do we need to know everything, the sum total of universal knowledge?" I will leave that question to you, to ponder on at your leisure, according to your own present level of awareness.

Yet, because of mankind's almost unquenchable thirst for knowledge, people do make the general assumption that a psychic adept like myself must know all the answers, must be the font of all knowledge, must be able to give out at a moment's notice a clear, concise, logical answer to virtually any question posed by one seeking to heighten their own level of awareness. The fact that this assumption is far removed from reality is one of the reasons why I refuse to be anyone's guru and even feel uneasy being described as a teacher. But there are adepts and even pseudoadepts who will quite readily encourage the assumption that they know everything, that they can answer every question put to them with a clarity and certainty that simply reinforces the cult status they are so eager to achieve and exploit.

It is reasonable and logical to assume that part of wanting all questions answered, all mysteries solved, for the universe and all creation to be placed in some orderly, third-dimensional manner that makes total sense to that individual at his or her present level of awareness, is the desire to remove every last vestige of fear. The fear of the unknown—perhaps man's most basic and oldest emotion.

Similarly, when I examine my own emotions, perhaps this is one of the reasons that explains my lack of complete knowledge with regard to my own psychic abilities and the awareness level they are capable of achieving. Perhaps there is a distant warning bell sounding within me, that if I choose to seek total awareness and gain it, I will somehow merge with the "Light" and, in doing so, lose my own individual, third-dimensional personality.

Therefore, what follows is a personal viewpoint of this "Light," which lies beyond the world that we know, even the world we are newly discovering within the psychic wilderness. I know, in writing this, that it is extremely unlikely that I, or anyone else in the foreseeable future, will be able to prove anything to anyone's great satisfaction regarding this subject.

I will lay before you the outer limits of my present awareness. I will reveal to you how far my psychic abilities have taken me and attempt to describe it in words, although, as I have already written in this book, sometimes the words we use are totally inadequate to describe what we know and feel. Perhaps you will be able to take my words and, using your own awareness, find the true essence of what I am trying to communicate.

It is now ten years since I was involved in lecturing and attempting to put ideas across to people, occasionally trying to provoke a positive reaction. When I retired in 1990 and came to Cyprus, I decided that I wished to remain anonymous. I had come to understand that there was little point in creating controversy or presenting a point of view that other people would not readily accept or could even comprehend. I felt that presenting my particular philosophies to people who were not of a like mind created argument, and I shied away from this.

I have looked into the mirror, as I have asked you to look into the mirror. I have looked far deeper than I am prepared to admit. I have reached a point of understanding now that if any skeletons were to come out of my cupboard, it would not disturb me. I would be able to face them and admit to what I did wrong and what I failed to do. I have looked at myself. I know myself and, yes, that is what causes me concern.

Let me try to explain. Medical science has recorded thousands of examples of what we term "near-death experiences." The descriptions have a remarkable similarity in that people who are near to death, whether through being involved in an accident or while they are being operated on in an operating theater, invariably describe a perception that they are traveling along a darkened tunnel or corridor, in some form of disembodiment. Many of these people realize they are experiencing something different when they feel their consciousness floating in the air and, when they look down, they see their body lying on the operating table.

These people say they feel they retain their senses, yet there is something very dreamlike about the feeling that their actions are not quite their own. They describe becoming aware of a blinding light at the end of the tunnel or corridor and experience a feeling of bewilderment, but an absence of fear. Some have even gone as far as saying that they were encompassed in a feeling of welcoming and contentment emanating from the light; a light that seemed to eradicate all fear and encouraged them to become part of the light.

They have spoken of seeing images of those that have died—relatives, loved ones—and that their desire to join them has been overwhelming.

During my lifetime of study and pursuit of knowledge, I have become aware of the reality of this Light of Awareness during my deepest meditations. Yet, I have most definitely shied away from entering it willingly. This must seem like a curious anomaly to the reader in that I present myself before you (despite my denial) as a teacher and yet now confess that I am reluctant to enter into this Light and gain from the awareness that it contains.

I have looked at myself totally and honestly and yet I feel curiously uneasy about this. I can look into that mirror and see myself and know myself. Yet, a part of my reasoning and logic argues with my awareness that those I have rejected, particularly those who subscribe to be mediums (an intermediary state between the two existences) could be right. After all, I am not infallible and have never claimed to be. So, logically, there must always exist that element of doubt that I could be wrong.

Using my awareness as my guide, I feel I am correct, and yet my intellect questions whether I could be wrong. If I am wrong, what then?

I have been asked on numerous occasions what my beliefs are regarding reincarnation. To me, reincarnation makes sense and is logical, being the continued evolution until such time as perfection is obtained. Some New Age theorists even go as far as stating, with absolute certainty, that the number of lifetimes we get is approximately 8,400,000. I, personally, cannot subscribe to this.

An analogy that I like and use during my lectures and seminars (although I do not totally ascribe to it) is that there are seven layers of existence beyond the physical, and that these seven layers are similar to sieves.

The first layer has a wide mesh and each subsequent layer has a finer mesh beneath it. Your level of awareness, or how many layers of grossness you have been able to remove before leaving the physical state, determines the size of mesh you are able to pass through, until you reach a point where you can go no further.

There seems to be little value in arriving at the point where you can go no further, to simply remain at this level, for you are still aware of there being something more.

What is of interest, however, is the theory that you can always go back through the layers and that you will reach a point where you have the opportunity to remove another coat of grossness. I believe that once we reach the final grid and are able to pass through it, there is no going back.

I no longer involve myself in any forms of psychic demonstrations. This is not to say that I may not do so at some point in the future. Perhaps I am looking for one that can really challenge me. I know now that I must ultimately face the greatest challenge of all—that of my own demise.

I have always felt the need to question even my own awareness and, as I have developed and began to formulate a new theory, I have continued to question what right I have in presenting these theories.

I have no concept of truth and of the ultimate truth. It must be quite clear to the reader that I have no belief in any spiritual pathway as such but I know that, ultimately, I face the greatest challenge to my present level of awareness.

For those who have a religious belief and are firmly entrenched within it, it must be fairly easy to face death, because theirs is a simple way when they die. According to the structure of life they have lived, this will determine where they are going, be it heaven or hell. I do not have these beliefs and therefore I cannot say that I look forward to death. But, until I reach that point of transition to what I will recognize, I think it is fair to say that they will have to drag me screaming and kicking along the darkened corridor toward the Light. This is because I know that ultimately I will become that which is,: and, in doing so, I will lose my own identity. And, surely, losing one's own identity is perhaps the object lesson to us all.

In essence, I cannot reject anything. If one merges with that Light, what does one become? What is beyond that? Is there a counterexistence following what is beyond the psychic wilderness?

We do not know. I do not know. But everything within me screams that there is no total extinction. I feel that if there is total separation from this illusory existence, it is because we need to advance to another illusory existence.

I would very much like to be part of the twenty-second century, because I believe that, by then, mankind will understand so much more. Equally, I hope that there will be a twenty-second century for mankind.

The reader might now be questioning what value there is in being psychic, in developing one's psychic ability, if fear prevents us from making the journey toward the Light of Awareness.

As I have argued throughout this book, I strongly believe that developing the psychic faculty and awareness is of tremendous value, inasmuch that my premise (and the way that I present it) is acceptable, we have by now perhaps created a bigger void than the one we began, having removed the solid security of religion as a barrier or an anchor. In creating this bigger phenomenon, is it possible that we have reinstated a sense of uneasiness, bordering on fear?

It seems a reasonable premise to suppose that accompanying each level of awareness is a level of fear. But, through the exercises in this book, one should be able to accept fear, come to terms with it and, eventually, turn it into a level of understanding. The process of turning relative fear into relative understanding is surely only developing awareness, by any other name.

In being able to present concepts of the original void and the psychic wilderness, I stated at the outset that words would become totally inadequate in an attempt to portray accurately something that defies the level of our descriptive powers. It is intangible. We have also emphasized that the more primitive a society, the greater the psychic ability and the greater the importance of this faculty, to be able to communicate on a psychic level and to recognize and react accordingly.

Man is believed by many to be the superior species of animal life that developed on the earth, our closest relative being the chimpanzee or ape. At some time in man's evolution, he began to recognize a means of communication—the spoken word. Our closest relative remains without this faculty. But, does it need it?

If you observe an animal (a cat or dog for example) you will see it suddenly transfixed, as though it is listening intently and staring in a certain direction. If you concentrate on this, you will become aware that it is feeling or perceiving something that may be totally invisible to the human eye, and that it is totally mesmerized by what it sees and hears.

There is no fear, but you can sense, without any question of doubt, the animal's bewilderment at what it is seeing, or sensing. It cannot communicate in what we would recognize as a sophisticated way, but it can respond. If you accidentally tread on its tail, for example, it will yelp. And our closest relatives still communicate by using a certain body language, beating on their chests and grunting.

At one time it was not necessary for our species to communicate in speech form but, at some point, it must have recognized the need to communicate in a more sophisticated way. Initially, the communication would have only been through a similar series of grunts, accompanied by some similar rudimentary body actions.

Science has now accepted that certain animal species communicate with each other on a more sophisticated level, that is, whales, through whale song, dolphins, through high-frequency sound emissions, and so forth. And primitive man must also have felt the need for a more sophisticated form of communication.

This need, or perhaps urge, to communicate in a more sophisticated way eventually took the form of languages. But this created a barrier, because without an identical frame of reference, there can be no exact translation between languages.

For instance, I once found myself in a situation where some legal documents, written in Greek, had to be translated into English. Some sentences would make no sense at all unless the translator rearranged their structure, so that, in its English form, it would communicate the exact meaning of the original documents for presentation in an English courtroom.

There is also the additional problem that some parts of one language have little or no direct meaning in another language. Remember my earlier story about the two frogs? One had never seen a tree and therefore, by lacking a common frame of reference, could not even conceive of what the other frog was trying to communicate. The problem within communication is the concept of truth. Relative truth. Absolute truth. This constant division. This, for me, is the intriguing question that we must strive to answer: Is there a point where, within human communication, there is a universal frame of reference?

Perhaps mankind should strive toward a universal language, Esperanto for instance, to be able to understand and cultivate the physical wilderness. It is interesting to note that the creators of the popular *Star Trek* science fiction series foresaw the need and development of a language called Standard, which everyone was taught on Earth and which served the travelers well when they went out into the galaxy to discover other life forms, because Standard was taught throughout the Galaxy.

Therefore, I have pondered on the question of presenting, in silence, an image for people of different languages to follow or meditate upon. If you could present one image, that is, the void, no-thing, it is far more recognizable and understandable than a thousand words.

I wonder whether there is a point at which we can communicate with one another, without any possible chance of misinterpretation? And, if I am correct, are we heading for a future generation that will accept the psychic faculty as fact and use this sixth sense with the same ease that they use their other five senses? Is this what the science fiction concepts refer to as telepathic communication, one with another, without any possible chance of misinterpretation? Can the truly developed psychic faculty become the universal frame of reference for us all?

One of my major worries about whether it will ever be possible to achieve this state is related to our physical world, the world within which we must be grounded. Mankind is constantly pumping into the world's atmosphere a vast array of man-made electromagnetic energies, radio waves, radiation, ionization, and communication transmissions. Orbiting satellites and high-powered transmitters and relay stations have virtually guaranteed that there is no escape from this anywhere in the world.

We may not fully understand precisely how everything works or whether there are side effects to all this energy we are giving out, but we know it is there, because the machines that we build work in the way we envisage they will.

In chapter one, we stressed that to have a clear understanding of nothing, broken down into no-thing, we should create a circle. By concentrating through meditation and, as a result of practicing the psychic development tape, this should now be quite easy for you to do. Therefore, if we look at this from a third-dimensional point of view, we can now accept the physical existence and embrace totally that the concept of past, present, and future has been in effect one; that we can now keep the confines of the circle there, but that we can break through and become at one with it.

But is it possible that, as a result of all the electromagnetic energies we are constantly pumping into our world, we have in fact created another circle? One which is totally invisible. It is not new; it has always been there, but as our intellect and technological achievements have grown, so we have localized it and in doing so, have created a greater barrier between third-dimensional concepts and the reality of no-thing. Does that have a contaminating effect on the psychic wilderness?

By removing the circle, we are back to the original state where all things were. We are now harnessing that energy and therefore we are localizing it.

What I would question is whether it is possible that the psychic energy field that exists all around us, like an atmosphere, is there for the benefit of all the species on the planet, and not just man? Is it possible that our man-made technological energies that we so casually release into our world are opening up not just slight chinks in the psychic wilderness, but gaping holes, holes similar to those that mankind has supposedly caused in the ozone layer and through which radiation from outer space pours.

Are we, in a similar manner, effectively polluting the psychic wilderness and, at the same time, building yet another barrier around ourselves that we must first strip away before gaining "clean" access to the psychic wilderness?

Those people I have developed personally through my psychic development seminars quickly appreciated why I stress, time and time again, the need for thorough cleansing before attempting to enter the psychic wilderness.

This cleansing takes the form of preparing an environment where you will not be disturbed for an hour and a half, disconnecting the telephone and making sure no one will physically disturb you. Eating a light meal at least an hour before your meditations is also essential, because if your digestive system is busily working away while you are meditating, this will also disturb you.

Bathing or showering is also essential to cleanse your body physically and psychologically, so that you can achieve a refreshed and relaxed state, wherein you can even forget the existence of the loose clothing you should be wearing.

One additional area of concern in cleansing the body is ridding oneself of the artificial electromagnetic energies that surround us and that saturate us in everyday modern life. These energies emanate from computers, telephones, cars, televisions—virtually every piece of modern machinery we encounter. Therefore, it is important to consciously try to "blow away" these artificial energies in the way that I described earlier in the book.

Certainly one of my concerns is whether it is possible that modern-day man has been creating gaping holes in the psychic wilderness through which energy is passing from the psychic wilderness into our third-dimensional world and vice versa. Could this be one of the reasons why mankind, in making a massive scientific technological leap in the last hundred years, is also making complementary but uneasy progress in its appreciation and knowledge of the psychic faculty?

Is it also possible that in creating gaping holes in the psychic wilderness, these holes open up at geographical locations in our third-dimensional world to which they are attracted, that is, the world's trouble spots, places where intense human conflict, destruction, famine, and suffering occur? Is there a symbiotic relationship between the world's trouble spots and holes in the psychic wilderness—a weak point, a doorway between the psychic wilderness and the third dimensional world through which symbiotic energies pass to and fro, feeding on one another and combining with one another, until we have a corrupted amalgam of these energies, swirling like a thundercloud within the psychic wilderness and within our third-dimensional world?

And, just as a thundercloud releases lightning bolts of energy, is it possible that these bolts of energy are attracted to weak points or conduits in the psychic wilderness and the third-dimensional world, and that they present a very real danger to both "worlds" and ultimately to mankind itself?

If this is the case, then clearly there is a very definite and necessary need for mankind to search for and apply acceptable standards of behavior in the world's trouble spots and tension points, or we run the risk of a chink in the psychic wilderness becoming a gaping hole, with all the attendant repercussions that could occur in both "worlds."

During the writing of this book, I have experienced and witnessed the most extraordinary sequence of events in relation to a fixed geographical location, and I feel it is something I must comment on, in an attempt to formulate a hypothesis on which I will base further investigation.

This book has been written in Cyprus during 1996. And it is fair to say that Cyprus became one of the world's hot spots during this year, bursting into prominence during the month of August, when violent clashes occurred along what is known as the Green line, the cease-fire line between the Greek-Cypriot part of the island in the south and the Turkish-occupied part of the island in the north, where the Turkish Cypriots live.

During the violent clashes, one Greek Cypriot was clubbed to death and another unarmed protester was shot and killed. Both killings were shown live on Cyprus television channels and the Greek Cypriots were shocked by the naked violence and hatred that came to the surface. The two factions came very close to war as a general armed mobilization took place on both sides.

I was on record as having predicted August's dramatic events many months earlier, expanding my prediction to include the repercussions of the events that took place in August.

During a television interview little more than a month later, I further predicted that the end of 1997 would bring about a positive result in Cyprus's problem, and at the end of 1997 there would certainly be more than just light at the end of the tunnel. Naturally, there was great interest expressed in this prediction by the television interviewer (and many other people) when the interview was transmitted.

Before the television interview, I was having dinner with some Cypriot friends and expressed my great interest in the Cyprus problem. I voiced my belief that there would be this Cyprus settlement by the end of 1997.

To my total surprise, my Cypriot friends declared with great passions: "Never."

I could not understand this completely negative attitude. Was it because they had lived so long with the problem that a general feeling of lethargy and negativity had created a totally negative force field? One that was impossible to penetrate without a greater understanding of the positive reality of the definite force that can be achieved by cultivating the psychic wilderness?

Is it possible that, in the main, Cypriot people have not yet broken free of the fetters and shackles of religion and sectarian belief and are unable to grasp the possibilities that those who have developed their awareness can so clearly see before them?

And, in the world's trouble spots, where the seriousness of war and deprivation is on a much larger scale than that of Cyprus, do those people face the even greater challenge of developing their awareness in a bubbling physical cauldron in order to find a solution to their problem?

My emergence on the Cyprus scene, along with other psychics, clairvoyants, and even Uri Geller, caused quite a strong reaction. It even provoked a spate of letters to the island's best-selling *Cyprus Weekly* newspaper, warning of the slippery slope to hell and eternal damnation if people should attempt to examine the psychic phenomenon or even seek to develop one's awareness. One letter writer saw only one solution: to return to the orthodox teachings of the church and reject all "foreign ideas that had polluted the island."

Is this the negative belief system that those of the orthodox religions of the world wish to set in stone to maintain their rigid grip and stranglehold on the societies in which they exist and rule not with an iron fist, but an iron mind?

Interestingly, a group of individuals, recognizing this problem in Cyprus, organized a "Pause For Peace" event, the first taking place on November 30, 1996. The idea was that, at a certain time on that day and other days, thousands of people would stop what they were doing and generate as many strong, positive thoughts as possible and project them islandwide to counteract the mood of negativity, cynicism, and depression that had built up on the island during the very tense year. The focal point was that people should concentrate on a united, peaceful Cyprus in 1997.

I believe it was an idea that definitely found its time, and it was interesting to note that for those people taking part and those who witnessed the event and subsequent events, it certainly had an uplifting effect and began to change the prevailing mood of the island. Perhaps by the time you are reading this book, a peaceful Cyprus settlement has come to pass and, if it has, surely this will be a historic example of what we, you and I, can achieve once we unlock the door and stride down the pathway unafraid.

By now, as a result of your own developing awareness, you should begin to grasp the concept that you are in control of your own destiny. I am positive in my belief that the more people begin to break away from the orthodox structures that exist in Cyprus and other trouble spots, the more they begin to think and feel for themselves, then the more positive effect and control they will have over their own lives.

Even we, in the so-called enlightened environment of this twentieth-century world, are still struggling and slowly winning the battle to overcome the political structures that have taken the part of religion as the immovable anchor, the vice-like grip on the mind.

Nowadays, we view life with a great deal more cynicism. Cynicism and a feeling of powerlessness are emotions that the establishment, be it political or religious, wants us to feel, to prevent us from slipping our anchor, slipping the shackles on our mind.

We must individually concentrate more and more on achieving personal awareness, and where we initially take the pathway to the discovery of the psychic self, a stronger human identity will also be created for us. We begin to identify and to realize that we are part of this universe. We are not any significant part, in terms of relative size, but we are an integral, conscious part of it, as it is part of us.

If we can cultivate the psychic wilderness and establish personal awareness, then we will begin to see quite clearly the positive statement that I made at the beginning—I am. The more people that become aware of that statement, the greater effect we can have on preventing this pollution, not only of the physical wilderness, but of the psychic wilderness also, a pollution that is affecting our very future. The Earth has been in existence for multimillions of years and we have progressed through evolution to our present point. Yet, I do not feel confident to predict a future for mankind that will last an equal length of time.

We are reaching the point where we have to recognize the slow destruction of our planet. But is it fair to say that *we* are destroying it? No, it is not. We, who are developing our awareness, are in the majority, yet we really have no say or control over our own destinies, because of our lack of political power. I believe we must continue to develop our awareness and consciously link up with other people who are equally committed to gaining control of their own destinies and, ultimately, the destiny of our planet and our race.

Perhaps the New Age has importance. My criticisms of gurus remain just as firm, but nonetheless, it is an interesting revolution of awareness that is taking place and the "New Ageists" are part of that revolution. The word revolution conjures up images of violence and militancy, but our revolution of awareness is a personal battle each and every one of us should seek to fight and win. There is no other way to cultivate the physical and psychic wilderness so that we may live at ease in both states.

I believe we are heading very rapidly toward a major breakthrough in scientific understanding, something radically new, a ground-breaking event.

To understand and comprehend the psychic wilderness, one has to concentrate on "no-thing," where the "norm" does not exist. It is impossible to be able to "live" within that environment without being firmly grounded and earthed in the physical world, the physical wilderness. One must complement the other, or we create an imbalance and then must attempt to exist within that state.

We should not be frightened of this new phenomenon and it should not deter us.

Consider this next example as a provocation of your growing awareness. The 1996 American presidential election campaign received blanket worldwide coverage, and I was somewhat stunned when I listened to a television trailer advertising a nonstop election coverage program of the November 5 election.

The casual announcement was to the effect that the

television station would broadcast coverage of the election all night with the question: "What does it mean for the rest of the world?"

I was not paying particular attention to the program at this time, but this casually delivered phrase caused quite a reaction within me. I immediately questioned why and how we, mankind, have created this situation where it has become assumed that one man can have such an overwhelming control over our lives?

Surely, this state of affairs is a denial of our awareness, if we allow it to be so. Surely, the people attending these election rallies must have realized in their hearts that the politician standing before them was only pretending to be "one of them" to gain their votes, and yet the vast majority of those people consciously let themselves be swept away by the hoo-ha of "the circus," losing sight of the fact that the whole thing was only a performance, a magic show, where nothing was of any real substance.

The mass media, particularly that of television, will happily cover the antics within the circus, because they only have one thing in mind—ratings. But if someone, even a journalist, should try to get up and put the politician on the spot with some intelligent questioning, he is likely to be surrounded by security people and ushered away and very likely to be blacklisted from future events. In this way, those that cling to the offices of power are able to dictate the terms and conditions under which we are allowed to view them and question them. They are allowed to paint the picture as they see it and we are forced to view or ignore it. Either way, the result is the same: the maintenance of the status quo. And we remain anchored, mortified, made to deny what we are.

We must strive to allow our own awareness to dictate to us how we live our lives and, in doing so and as our awareness grows, we will possibly develop a greater power in refusing to allow this one man to come to power.

When we are confronted with this casual assumption (even drip-drip brainwashing) that we are helpless before the power that is wielded by one man, we must seek to break free from these psychological shackles that attempt to render us helpless and remember that it is our life. If we do not seek awareness, what do we have left?

In truth, we cannot know personally this man who seeks to become the president of the United States of America. We are only allowed to see his carefully crafted public image and hear his diligently rehearsed sound bites of wisdom, which will be written for him by a team of experienced speechwriters catering to the needs of the audience.

Yet, as we ourselves, in our own personal development, have had the courage to face the mirror of self-discovery and to look at ourselves and at who we really are, we know that this one man is not extraordinary in any particular respect. He is simply a man seeking political power. And his only talent may be in his expertise over his opponent at playing the coast-to-coast political circus of electioneering in the United States of America. The best player of the game wins the prize, although in this case it is the ultimate prize—the power of life or death over the world's population. That is the reality of the world we have created and allowed to remain in existence. That is the reality that your awareness will reveal to you. I wonder what is the extent of the man's knowledge? What secrets is he privy to that are denied to the rest of us? Why is it necessary for him to have ultimate power and to deny us knowledge?

In this respect, it has been widely rumored for many years now that the United States has recovered, and keeps in top security storage, an alien spacecraft complete with its alien pilots. And it is suggested that it is not necessary for the rest of the world to know this. Why? Because it would destroy everything that we are expected to believe in and build our lives upon. Would those with strictly defined religious beliefs suddenly find everything they have been taught to believe cast into doubt? If religious beliefs teach that God created man, and just man, then who or what created the extraterrestrials? And, if these extraterrestrials had a religious faith, who would their God be?

The revelation that intelligent life exists in places other than the Earth could prompt a mass desertion from the organized religions. Millions of people worldwide would suddenly cut themselves loose from their religious anchors and seek greater personal awareness and understanding. This revolution of awareness would surely send shockwaves through the political, social, and religious establishments. It would probably cause them to collapse into obsolescence, and many, many people who are protecting their own self-interests of power and wealth would not want that to happen. But, eventually, happen it must, because the revolution of awareness is here. It is growing exponentially, as one teacher develops ten students, who in turn become teachers themselves, each with ten students, ad infinitum, and the establishment knows that there is little they can do to stop it. They can only delay the revolution of awareness by using various distractions, like encouraging the unthinking pursuit of materialism that binds people to the established ways of the world.

It is fairly obvious to date that as our intellect and awareness has grown, it is not necessary to question the existence or deny the existence of God, for it is painfully obvious that he is impotent within our third-dimensional existence.

Perhaps God would have had greater power over us and our destiny had we not evolved, as discussed in chapter one, in the book of Genesis, when God asked Adam why he hid from Him. Adam replied that it was because he realized he was naked. Perhaps you can now understand the significant statement made in chapter one when God allegedly said: "Who told you, you were naked? "Who gave man this knowledge? Wasn't this the moment when God became impotent because mankind had developed its own awareness?

Our world can only be but a speck of dust in the eye of what we conceive to be the ultimate being—power, or God. It is an irritant to be washed away when one considers the total concept.

When mankind first looked to the stars, it became inevitable that one day it would need to develop a system of measurement that could be used to quantify the distance between Earth and the stars that he sought to understand. Using advanced mathematics, the scientist was eventually able to calculate the distance between the Earth and the nearest star to Earth (excluding our Sun, which is 93 million miles away from us). But the scientist could not keep repeating that the nearest star, Proxima Centauri, is 25.2 trillion miles away. Most calculators do not have enough digit spaces to work this out. Rather, the scientist, for ease of calculation and human understanding and comprehension, developed a measurement system using light-years. That is, if the speed of light is 186,200 miles per second, it would take a beam of light 4.2 light-years to reach Proxima Centauri.

In truth, we cannot even imagine this distance because we cannot really imagine (as yet) something moving at a speed of 186,200 miles a second when earthbound machines like the F15 fighter plane has a top speed of Mach 2.5, which is only 1,900 miles per hour.

The bright star Rigel in the constellation Orion is a mere 880 light years away; Deneb in Cygni only 1,630 light-years distant; and the famous spiral galaxy M31 in the constellation Andromeda lies a colossal 2,200,500 light-years away—12.9 quintillion miles. It is a remarkable thought that the light from M31 can be seen with the naked eye in the night sky but that that light reaching Earth left M31 centuries ago; has taken all that time to travel, at 186,200 miles a second; and is just reaching us now.

The *Star Trek* series gave us an inkling of understanding that if we could ever build spacecraft to travel at warp speed, faster than the speed of light, then perhaps mankind could get over the hurdle of vast, unimaginable distances. Of course, even with the *Star Trek* concept, and with the ability to travel at these warp speeds, it still took months of space travel to get from one destination to another, hence the initial premise of a five-year mission away from Earth.

Space is so vast that perhaps mankind will never completely chart its regions, in terms of physically traveling these distances. But that does not mean that it may not be possible to explore these realms, using developed awareness.

Once again, we are getting to the point where words fail to describe what we "see" and comprehend with our developed awareness, but through constant practice with your psychic development tape and a deeper search for all that is within us, you will begin to understand the energy, the power, that is there for each and every one of you to tap into, to explore, even to marvel at, in the same way a young child will view, with innocent delight, its first fireworks display.

There is no fear, no misunderstanding; and perhaps no genuine comprehension at first. But, just like the child, you will begin to learn and make perfect sense of what you "see" before you and what you experience.

How dare those who cling to power and are blinded by it, be they priest or president, dictate to us how we should live our lives, particularly at this time when the protection of our planet and environment is vitally important to us all.

Consider this paradox. There are many, many people who do not want to even consider the very real possibility of universal global destruction. There are others, now a very real and growing number, who in seeking and achieving awareness, could not care less either way, because they know they are going to achieve continued existence. Hence, the motivation behind my earlier statements that it is essential that we should seek to live at ease in both the physical and psychic wilderness, to straddle both environments in an attempt to achieve a harmony, a unity, a duality between these two very real states of existence.

Are the statements I am now making bordering on the advocacy of anarchy, or are they proof of an awareness and acknowledgment of my own personal responsibilities?

Do we remain complacent in the belief that we are just an irritant in the eye of God, who has total knowledge, and do nothing because of our helplessness? Or do we break the fetters of convention and become part of what is, what was, and what will be?

The destruction of Earth by our own actions might never be total, but it could give rise to a second Genesis.

Perhaps the most urgent thing to become aware of here is when the presidents, prime ministers, and priests try to retain control or dominate our lives, I believe they are no different to those establishment men of 2,000 years ago, who were challenged by the wisdom and courage of one man who attempted to teach us all. Yet, he became a political and religious threat.

Now, because of the more sophisticated times we live in, I wonder how many people who have discovered truths that are unpleasant to the establishment have been systematically "eased out" of the mainstream of society, suddenly losing their jobs or having their reputations tarnished in some way, accused of being maladjusted—even a danger to society?

How many of us, who seek awareness in the twentieth century, have been crucified in some way for our pursuit of "the truth." And, more to the point, for how much longer can the political and religious establishment keep back the tidal wave of consciousness that is sweeping the planet and that will eventually sweep them away totally?

A closer analysis of Christianity, which is a comparatively new belief system (being only 2,000 years old) reveals many predictions of a better world, a better existence, and yet, for 2,000 years, we have sat in complacency, waiting for either the deliverance or for the New Messiah, without realizing that there is no individual messiah that will come and offer us this deliverance.

We have already been given everything. It is up to us to find our deliverance, our messiah within, first as individuals, then collectively, without falling into the trap of rejecting one sectarian belief and substituting it with another. That is the biggest danger.

If you reject the structure of society as it exists and, with other like-minded people, remove yourselves from society and form a sect (and we have seen many examples of this), you are courting the same disaster as that which has befallen many, if not all of these groups. They are dismissed as cranks, even though their ideas and principles and reasoning may be totally sound. But they fall into the trap of rejecting one society and forming another—and rejection is a negative energy.

In achieving a breakthrough and achieving psychic

awareness, we now begin to look at the possibility of changing the term "psychic awareness" quite simply to that of "awareness of oneself."

I believe it is possible that the future could well hold not societies, as such, but people who have achieved awareness and who no longer need a structure or organized society. Their own awareness enables them to be able to live at peace one with another.

We talk of our present achievements as being a result of past pioneers. We talk of men of vision and foresight. At the time of their existence they were indeed pioneers and they did have vision. Where are the men of vision today? Is it the scientists? All things now are seemingly possible.

Within the past fifty years, tremendous strides have been made. Even during the writing of this book, scientists believe they have found primordial signs of life on Mars and even a new planet, hundreds of light-years away.

Astronomers always believed the star Capella in the constellation Auriga was simply that—one star. But, as a result of technological progress, using computer-enhanced radio telescopes, they have now established that Capella is in fact two stars.

Computers are now able to construct a virtually exact facsimile of any one individual, even to the point that, at a future time, the computer disk can be reactivated.

Scientists have conducted extensive research in the field of cryogenics, where it is believed that in the near future it will be possible to freeze our life-forms and preserve them in a state of suspended animation and, many years later, to successfully reactivate these bodies without any ill effects. The reasoning behind such research is that medical conditions that are incurable now may become treatable in fifty years time.

We can thank the scientific and medical communities for their work that has resulted in average life expectancies rising to around the age of seventy years and above. Perhaps in the next century, the average life expectancy may reach 100?

The scientific community is composed of people with very strict standards of morals and ethics and I believe that, at all times, when they investigate and study future developments to enhance both life and mankind generally, they do try to embrace moral concepts.

Certainly, within the field of cryogenics, they must have looked at this concept of the human soul, and possibly come to the same understanding that I have—that there is no such thing as the individual soul and that, once the physical body dies, the person becomes part of the psychic wilderness. The question is whether it is not beyond the realms of possibility that the individuality of the person can somehow be rejoined with the reactivated body?

I am firmly of the opinion that the demise of the individual in the physical form is exactly that—that his or her individuality join forces and become part of a positive energy field that can be tapped by future generations. I cannot subscribe to the idea of regeneration of a body kept alive by cryogenics. To do so is to conjure up visions of the modern Frankenstein's monster, a body that is alive in the physical sense but most certainly is not inhabited by its original personality. The body would be without that vital original spark and we can only speculate as to the dangers of what might try to occupy the empty human shell.

Would not regenerating life and expecting the original personality to still be there be equivalent to dabbling with the energy forces of the psychic wilderness by using a Ouija board?

Surely, it is logical to assume that just because we

have some understanding of how to reactivate a physical body through the process of cryogenics, this certainly does not give us any understanding of whether it is possible to reactivate a departed personality—and, if it is possible, whether "forcing" the personality back into its physical form after it has joined with the psychic wilderness, would not expose mankind as a whole to forces, and possibly dangers, we cannot understand and may not know how to control?

I have thought about this subject at great length and these are my perceptions, derived from my current level of awareness. It is not my intention to create confusion at the end point of your first journey on the road to psychic awareness and eventually, to complete awareness.

I hope that at this point, your own awareness level is sufficiently developed for you to be able to grasp the possible dangers I perceive in letting our drive for scientific knowledge go unchecked, without an accompanying forward movement in our understanding and awareness of ourselves, our human spirit, our personalities, our psyche.

The exercises in this book have been created only to bring you to a certain point where you can recognize the psychic faculty and use it at a very simple and basic level. As to where you take it, where you go to from here, that is entirely up to you.

Let your own awareness be your guide. It can only be hoped that you have achieved this point of awareness. You know you can enter into the wilderness; you know you have entered into the wilderness. You know that you are perfectly safe and that there is nothing to fear. I cannot predict where you will go from here.

Appendix I Psychic Realities
Audio Side One

(Music)

Come, let us take our first steps together into that which is known as meditation. Not a world of mystery, nothing to fear. We are simply going to cross from the conscious state into the reality of your inner self. You want to be aware from the instructions given, of the necessity to have eaten a balanced meal so that your body is not concentrating on digesting or feeling the necessity for food. You have bathed, you have taken the necessary precautions to prevent any disturbance, the removal of the telephone receiver. You are completely alone, we are together, my voice is all you hear. Allow my voice to be the control. Try to avoid an intellectual reaction to what I say. Allow the words simply to flow over you. Follow instructions. You have now entered into the first stage. Let us relax. The word "relax" is the most difficult to understand when you are attempting to concentrate upon that which I speak. So, allow your focal point to be the natural rhythm of your breathing. Concentrate only upon that, the gentle rhythmic breathing, in and out, in and out. That is all.

Now, allow your eyelids to become slightly heavier, still focusing your attention on the natural rhythm of your breathing. Feel the tension and dross begin to leave your body. Take your concentration now to the top dead-center of your head. There, imagine a hole.

Now take your concentration to the center of the forehead and imagine another hole. Now to the center of the throat and imagine another hole; to the center of the heart, again imagine there is a hole; to the center of the spleen, which is centered directly in line with the heart at the bottom under the rib cage. Now take your concentration to the solar plexus. There is no need to imagine a hole here, for it is already there. This is the center of vibration, which we all feel. It is the center you have read about where we all naturally react. The center of gross vibrations; the center of anticipation or of bad news being imminent. When we say "I have butterflies in my stomach," when we feel something unpleasant is about to happen it is all emanating from the center of the solar plexus.

So, take your concentration away from the center and slowly draw your attention up toward the center of the forehead, breathing in. Concentrate now upon the center of the forehead. Focus your whole attention on it. Now, relax. Fall, once again, into the rhythm of your breathing. You may feel slightly tense. You may have a slight sensation around the center of your forehead. Do not be concerned but analyze that which you feel.

Become used to noticing subtle changes which take place as you progress during each exercise.

Gauge your own reaction toward these changes. It is that hidden psychic faculty operating, that psychic faculty which lies dormant within each and every person, that faculty which is the ability to see and recognize, that which lies beyond normal perception. There is no mystery, so relax. Concentrate upon the natural rhythm of your breathing and begin to feel the silence, the strange stillness. Allow my voice only to create the image, but remember I am not your teacher. I am simply your guide. So, together, let us take a further step.

Concentrate once again on the center of the forehead. Do not be concerned at any sensation that you experience. If it becomes too oppressive, then simply relax. At all times, should you feel uncomfortable because something is happening that makes you slightly nervous, remember the key word "relax." Concentrate only on the natural rhythm of your breathing. That is all you need to do.

Now imagine that you are in the desert. You are all alone, surrounded by sand. The heat of the sun is oppressive. You look for shelter. All around you is sand. You can only feel the oppressive heat of the sun reflecting upon this sand. From the center of your forehead, look directly ahead of you. See the gradual form of a palm tree gradually taking shape. Through the leaves of the palm tree, see the shimmering water. Visualize an oasis. Go into that oasis. As you enter the welcoming shade, you begin to feel relief from the oppression of the desert. Relax. See the cool, clear water. There is nothing else but you, encompassed by the soothing shade of the palm trees, refreshed by the coolness that reflects from the water. Relax. Feel yourself being immersed into this refreshing cool water. That is all. There is nothing but peace. Nothing.

(Meditating)

Allow my voice to gently break into the peace you have been experiencing, to bring you back to your conscious reality. Feel the vibrations that have been created by your entering into meditation. Bring your focal point once again to the natural rhythm of your breathing. Let us analyze what it is that we have tried to achieve with our first step. The desert is the symbol of our environment. Our normal day-to-day life. We are accustomed to living within the hustle and bustle of that environment. We do not accept or acknowledge the pressures which force us to earn a living, to relate to other people, to travel backwards and forwards to our place of work. It becomes part of our natural, physical existence. And therefore, the question of being able to relax is extremely difficult. The oasis is at all times the place you can enter. It is your own choice. My voice only assisted you in creating the image.

Is it illusion or reality? Is the reality that which you experience daily while your conscious involvement in your physical life? Or is the reality that which you experienced as you sat at the oasis? How do you now feel? How is your body? Allow time to determine the answers, but remember they are there and you have but taken the first step. We began by opening our chakras. We must now close them. So, concentrate on each center as I name them. And close down that imaginary hole which you have created by mentally placing a cross over each center. The top dead-center of the head; the center of the forehead; the center of the throat; the center of the heart; the center of the spleen, and the center of the solar plexus. Now, as you sit, take an imaginary line from underneath your left foot. Bring it up around the left-hand side of your body, breathing in as you do so. Bring the line to the top of the head and then continue down the right-hand side of your body, breathing out. Take the line down underneath your right foot, symbolically enclosing the whole of your body with this imaginary line. You have been sitting for some time, possibly unaware of the time which has passed. If you have not been successful the first time, do not be concerned. Persevere and you will achieve the image.

Now, become aware of your physical body. Wiggle your toes. Feel the sensation of your own body and bring your concentration up from your feet to your knees, to your trunk, your chest, and finally to your head. Gently wiggle your fingers and, in your own time, open your eyes. Analyze the vibrations you feel in the room where you sit. Analyze how you feel. Do not be in too much of a hurry to become involved in doing something. Remain for a while, contemplating and analyzing how you feel. Concentrate with this exercise on a daily basis until such time as you are ready for the next step.

(Meditating)

Appendix 2 Psychic Realities Audio Side Two

(Music)

Let us now take the next step. There is no necessity to repeat the instructions. By now you should have become fairly adapt in the primary stages of meditation. You are aware of the peace which you can experience within the oasis. You know how to prepare yourself, so let us begin.

Relax. Once again, this is the trigger to concentrate upon the natural rhythm of your breathing. In and out. Let that be your whole focal point. There is not necessity to open the chakras. Having practiced meditation with side one of this tape many times, the chakras will automatically open. For this next stage there is no necessity to concentrate upon any one chakra.

We are now attempting to enter into an understanding of the psychic faculty. That which is dormant within you. There is no mystery and yet, to help you to achieve it, the only medium that is available is that of words, words which can confuse and conflict with your own preconceived ideas or concepts of philosophy. It is extremely difficult to overcome these natural prejudices when being introduced to that with which you disagree. Simply allow my voice to create images. Try to avoid your intellect being uppermost and analyzing that which is said. We must begin at one point. Though in truth there is no beginning. The majority of you have been brought up to accept and understand a very basic religious teaching of your environment. Let us take what is perhaps the most important aspect of that teaching, one that is perhaps not fully understood, that which is contained within the book of Genesis. The beginning.

It is not my intention to create or destroy any image that you may have of that which is termed "God." I will, however, suggest that Genesis gives the opportunity to have a greater understanding and pass through that veil which has been created in you by the introduction of secular belief. Genesis begins thus, "In the beginning was the word and the word was God. And the earth was dark and without form." This may seem in itself to be a contradiction. If there was no form, then how can one visualize a third dimension such as Earth. It indicates that in the beginning was nothing. But there is no such thing as nothing. For nothing indicates something.

Remember, this is not an intellectual exercise. As you concentrate, picture a blank space. If questioned "what do you see?" your intellectual answer would be nothing. And yet it is something. To understand it, let us break down nothing to be no-thing. No-thing. The beginning. To understand this even greater, create a circle within the visual state of no-thing. What do you see and recognize? A circle.

What is in the center of the circle? No-thing—it is outside of the circle. Which is the reality? Which is the illusion? Is it not possible that reality is that which is there and always will be? No-thing. And the illusion is that which you have created the circle, which is encompassing that no-thing. But to remove the circle would place an impossible burden upon those who need the psychological crutch of a third-dimensional understanding. I say we are all psychic. It is within us. It is part of us. And yet psychologically it is difficult to cross that gulf between the reality of no-thing and the illusion of something.

Now relax. Just simply allow the rhythm of your breathing to become your focal point. Now you must begin to analyze your feelings, your reactions. You are not in what can be termed "a normal situation." Your eyes are closed. Images are being created for you. But what do you feel? Remember your first exercise, which is simply to enable you to relax, to begin to experience the inner self, to relieve yourself of stress and anxiety, to overcome the discomforts of the physical self much the same as now. You are having a reaction. Analyze that reaction. Do not allow it to disturb you, for there is nothing. You are entering into that state which is known as vibrations. Just relax. Now slowly begin to enhance your breathing so that you are taking in slightly deeper breaths and slightly deeper still. Now you are concentrating much more upon your breathing. Allow it to slow down to its natural rhythm and bring your concentration up to your eyes. Concentrate upon your eyes. They are closed. Just concentrate upon them. Your eyes are what you use each and every day automatically to visualize all that is contained within your third-dimensional existence. You understand the concept of the third dimension and you use your eyes to relay that which you see for your brain to interpret. In concentrating upon your eyes, imagine them as two holes. Concentrate on looking through those holes. You are not using your eyes. You are looking through them and you cannot be involved in any third-dimensional reality.

This exercise should help you embrace the concept of the inner self. So, now relax. You should experience a slight sensation around the eyes—maybe a slight sensation of pressure around the head. So, spend more time relaxing into the natural of rhythm of your breathing. That's fine. You are relaxed. The vibrations are still. You are at one with no-thing. Remember the symbol of the oasis and the cool, clear water. It was still, transparent. You could see through to the bottom without disturbance. If you were to drop a stone into this water, it would distort and cause ripples. It would prevent you from seeing clearly. Seeing clearly; clairvoyance. Clear vision. It is there; you have this ability. The faculty has been dormant and now you have awakened it. But that which you see is not of a third-dimensional state. Again, analyze how you feel. What is this strange vibration in which you find yourself?

Let us be free. Let us enjoy freedom. Allow your mind to roam. Imagine a white horse. Place the horse wherever you will. Now set the horse to run. It is free. It is unbridled. There are no restrictions. See the horse's ears pricked up and the wind blowing through its mane. Become that horse. Be free.

(Meditating)

Having roamed free, now become aware of your physical body. Wiggle your toes. If you have achieved freedom with the horse, the sensation of the vibration of becoming aware of your physical body should be quite definite. What have you experienced? Note the subtle changes of vibration as your analytical mind now becomes aware of your physical body. Take a deep breath. Hold it—and exhale. Rotate the head slightly. Now it is your physical body you are aware of. So, let us close the chakras with the cross as we have learned to do. The top dead-center of the head. The center of the forehead. The center of the throat. The center of the spleen. The center of the solar plexus. Before you finalize closing your aura, it is important that you understand for the next exercise how important it is to protect this aura which emanates all around you.

(Clap)

Relax. Relax. How do you feel? Are you not disturbed? Jangling? We have a dropped a stone into the pool of water and disturbed the whole thing. It is important that always, from now on, you prepare yourself to experience vibrations that can disturb, not in a way that is detrimental, but once you open yourself up and enter into this environment where vibration exists, you must protect yourself and close down. It will take a little time now for your body to stop jangling. So close down your aura by concentrating on a point underneath your left foot, bringing the line up around the left side of your body, breathing in until you reach the top dead-center of your head and continue down the right-hand side, breathing out. Take a deep breath. Wiggle your fingers slightly and in your own time open your eyes and spend some time analyzing your reaction to what you have experienced.

How to Purchase this Tape

Copies of this tape are available by contacting the author at:

Atlas Printing Company, Ltd.
P.O. Box 50503
3606 Limassol, Cyprus
Telephone/fax: 05-362911
E-mail: atlas1@cytanet.com.cy

Substitute numbers for the letters above
by using the following code:

EVOLVE
123421

LEOV

About the Author

Bob Cracknell is a natural psychic, having had his first psychic experience at the age of seven years. He came to prominence in the early '70s and achieved academic acclaim from the Oxford University Society of Psychic Research, by scoring an 80 percent accuracy rating in an experiment in precognition and remote viewing.

He achieved notoriety by openly challenging the Spiritualist establishment's claims that all mediums are controlled by guides—and that their abilities are gifts.

As his reputation grew, he became fascinated by criminal mysteries and assisted the police in various countries, giving psychic clues. His notable successes include the "Yorkshire Ripper" case, the Janie Shepherd murder case, and others, all described by Colin Wilson in Cracknell's autobiography, *Clues to the Unknown.* To quote Colin Wilson, ". . . something completely new in the strange field of the paranormal. He is one of the most interesting psychics alive today. . . ."

In the '70s, as a result of his psychic involvement in helping the police, he became known as Britain's Number-One Psychic Detective. He formed an international organization, tracking down criminals throughout the world. He became a member of IPI and IAATI, an organization of law enforcement officers, under the control of the FBI, and has written a book dealing with these cases.

He has lectured extensively and has been the subject of numerous television interviews and profiles.

Bob Cracknell is no longer active in this field and now lives in the beautiful Mediterranean Island of Cyprus, with his wife, Jenny, devoting his time to writing.